First-Century Christlikeness in a 21st-Century Time

Dr. Charles Lee Wilson and Kay Moore

CrossHouse

Published by
CrossHouse Publishing
PO Box 461592
Garland, TX 75046-1592

Printed in the United States of America
by Lightning Source, LaVergne, TN
Cover design by Dennis Davidson

ISBN 978-1-934749-41-8
Library of Congress Control Number 2009920282

Contents

Preface

Looking at the first-century church in its infancy is one of the best ways we have of analyzing how we can do a better job of having Christ-centered congregations and evaluating how well we are doing enacting biblical objectives for the church. The New Testament is full of illustrations of how those in the early church were admonished to conduct themselves in relationship to one another. We can benefit from looking at how these first-century Christians were instructed and then by applying these teachings to our 21st-century lives.

In the pages that follow are 13 lessons. Each examines one facet of the New Testament's "one-another" teachings. In your small-group time for the each of next 13 weeks you will study one of the "one-another" admonishments. Begin your study with lesson 1.

Preceding the lessons is an introduction on page 7 that provides background for the 13-week study. It is an explanation of what the church is to be about. It tells why the church exists and what its objectives and mandates are. I highly encourage you to read this introduction for your own personal edification before you begin your actual study in lesson 1, page 27. Some questions for your consideration appear at the end of the introduction. These are for your personal devotional time only. However, thinking about possible answers to them will greatly enhance your application of the material that follows.

At the end of each lesson you will find some questions for study. Review these and be prepared to discuss these matters when your small group convenes weekly.

I have been privileged to write the main study material for each week's lesson; veteran curriculum writer Kay Moore has provided the study questions (and separately, helps for leaders.)

I pray that God will guide your study as you proceed through these next 13 weeks. May He use this concentrated time to advance His kingdom.

Dr. Charles Lee Wilson, Pastor
Sunnyvale First Baptist Church
Sunnyvale, TX

Introduction

The Church's Purpose and Priorities

Socrates was wise, some have said, not because he knew the right answers, but because he knew how to ask the right questions. Of all questions, perhaps none delves to the depths of an issue faster than does the question, "*Why*?"

The Old Testament is replete with penetrating *why's*. God asks Cain, "*Why are you angry?*" The Lord asks Abraham, "*Why did Sarah laugh?*" Moses asks, "*Why is the bush not burned up?*" Nathan asks David, "*Why have you despised the Word of the Lord?*" Job asks, "*Why did I not die at birth?*"

As we turn to the New Testament, "*Why?*" seems to be Jesus' favorite question. We see Him asking, "*Why are you anxious? Why do you look at the speck in your brother's eye? Why do you call Me, Lord, Lord, and do not do what I say? Why do you not believe Me? Why have you forsaken Me?*"

The question "*Why?*" has a way of tearing through the superficial husk of a matter and shucking right down to the cob. The "*Why?*" we ask today is no exception. "Why does the church exist?" The question is one of purpose. When all extras are set aside—when we dig right down to the tap-root reason for our being on earth at this time—what do we find is the true purpose of the church?

Scripturally, we as the church have two reasons for our existence:

1) The Great Commandment. "'*Teacher, which is the great commandment in the law?' Jesus said to him, 'You shall love the Lord your God with all your heart, with all your soul, and with all your mind.' This is the first and great commandment. And the second is like it: 'You shall love your neighbor as yourself.' On these two commandments hang all the Law and the Prophets*" (Matt. 22:36-40).

2) The Great Commission. "*Go therefore and make disciples of all the nations, baptizing them in the name of the Father and of the Son and of the Holy Spirit, teaching them to observe all things that I have commanded you; and lo, I am with you always, even to the end of the age*" (Matt. 28:19-20).

I. Four major objectives of the church

The church has four main objectives. To gain insight into how we are to accomplish these objectives, we look back to the church in its infancy. In Acts 2, we see four pictures of the church in its embryonic form. From these pictures, we will be able to determine the major objectives of any local assembly that springs into existence. These objectives are cross-cultural, cross-denominational, and true in spite of the ministry's style or size. They are the specific avenues through which we are to carry out the purpose of the two pillars of the Great Commandment and the Great Commission. Think about the life of your own local congregation as you study these objectives.

> 42 *And they continued steadfastly in the apostles' doctrine and fellowship, in the breaking of bread, and in prayers.*
>
> 43 *Then fear came upon every soul, and many wonders and signs were done through the apostles.*
>
> 44 *Now all who believed were together, and had all*

things in common,
45 *and sold their possessions and goods, and divid-*
ed them among all, as anyone had need.
46 *So continuing daily with one accord in the tem-*
ple, and breaking bread from house to house, they ate
their food with gladness and simplicity of heart,
47 *praising God and having favor with all the peo-*
ple. And the Lord added to the church daily those who
were being saved (Acts 2:42-47).

Objective A: Love

Looking at verse 42 we get the mental picture of a body of committed, worshipful people. The Greek term meaning "to devote" is also used in Acts 1:14 and 6:4. It connotes a steadfast, single-minded fidelity. For the early church, worship is not a half-hearted effort; it is intense, but it holds a beautiful simplicity—the breaking of bread and prayer. Yet amid those simple expressions of worship is a profound reverence, as Acts 2:43 indicates: *Everyone kept feeling a sense of awe*. The Greek states simply, *And came to every soul, fear.* No one truly worships who doesn't possess a healthy and awesome respect for the most high, most holy God. Verse 46 suggests a unity in the worship, *So continuing daily with one accord in the temple, and breaking bread from house to house, they ate their food with gladness and simplicity of heart . . .*.

Again, here we see, as also shown in the Greek, *simplicity of heart*. Worship is basic and glad, not morbid and sophisticated. When you're finished worshiping, the experience is designed to equip you to feel clean and fresh—ready to face the challenges God has placed before you.

The goal of worship is to exalt the name of Jesus.

> 19 *What am I saying then? That an idol is anything, or what is offered to idols is anything?*
> 20 *Rather, that the things which the Gentiles sacrifice they sacrifice to demons and not to God, and I do not want you to have fellowship with demons . . ..*
>
> 31 *Therefore, whether you eat or drink, or whatever you do, do all to the glory of God* (1 Cor. 10:19-21; 31).

Even though the New Testament throbs with consuming purpose to glorify God, our post-modern phase grows faint on this point. Our hearts beat more in rhythm with corporate America than with the early church—more with Madison Avenue than with the manuscripts of the New Testament—more with Broadway and its performance than with a bowed, humble heart before a holy God. We think in terms of numerical growth rather than personal growth. Our goal is often to make an impression in worship—to achieve the "ah-ha" moment with its emotional "warm fuzzies" than to be broken in the presence of our Blessed Lord and Savior.

> 11 *Therefore we also pray always for you that our God would count you worthy of this calling, and fulfill all the good pleasure of His goodness and the work of faith with power,*
> 12 *that the name of our Lord Jesus Christ may be glorified in you, and you in Him, according to the grace of our God and the Lord Jesus Christ* (2 Thess. 1:11-12).

Note the reciprocal action in these verses. As you glorify God, you will be glorified in Him. When others observe your life, they will want to glorify Him also, just as Matthew 5:16b affirms: "*Let your light shine before men in such a way that they may see your good works, and glorify your Father who is in heaven.*"

To glorify means to magnify or elevate, shedding radiance or splendor to another. *To glorify God* means to magnify and elevate the Lord as we diminish and deny ourselves. This is best illustrated by the words of John the Baptist, who says, "*he must increase, but I must decrease*" (John 3:30). John is the voice (1:23); Jesus is the Word (1:14). John is only a man; Jesus is the Messiah. John does not even consider himself worthy to untie the strings of Jesus' shoes. Glorifying God in worship means being occupied with and committed to God's ways rather than preoccupied with and determined to accomplish our own ways.

> 2 "*Why do you spend money for what is not bread, and your wages for what does not satisfy? Listen carefully to Me, and eat what is good, and let your soul delight itself in abundance . . ..*
>
> 8 *For My thoughts are not your thoughts, Nor are your ways My ways, says the Lord.*
> 9 *For as the heavens are higher than the earth, so are My ways higher than your ways, and My thoughts than your thoughts*" (Isa. 55:2; 8-9).

> 1 *I will extol You, my God, O King; and I will bless Your name forever and ever.*
> 2 *Every day I will bless You, and I will praise Your name forever and ever* (Ps. 145:1-2).

Have you ever tried doing that? Have you ever exalted the Lord in the explicit and enthusiastic way that the psalm you just read describes? Of course, praising the Lord when you have the wind at your back and you are sailing smoothly along is easy, but what about the times the wind is whipping you in the face? Can you give glory to Him in worship then? Take a look at another time in David's life when the bottom dropped out and he had nowhere to look but up. Note the same spirit of praise.

> 1 *"Incline thine ear, O Lord, and answer me, for I am afflicted and needy.*
> 2 *Do preserve my soul, for I am a godly man; O thou my God, save thy servant who trusts in thee . . ..*
>
> 7 *In the day of my trouble I shall call upon thee, for thou will answer me"* (Ps. 86:1-2; 7).

Recognize this: In the day of his trouble, David calls on the Lord. In the day of your trouble, on whom do you call? In the day of financial trouble, do you try to "master the possibilities" with your credit cards, or do you call on the Master? In the day of trouble in finding God's will, do you seek out only the counsel of other people? Or first and foremost, do you seek out the one whose name is *Wonderful, Counselor, Prince of Peace*?

David sings praises to God instead of "singing the blues."

> 8 *"There is no one like thee among the gods, O Lord; nor are there any works like Thine . . ..*
> 10 *For Thou art great and doest wonderful deeds; Thou alone art God.*
> 11 *Teach me Thy way, O Lord; I will walk in thy*

truth; unite my heart to fear Thy name.

12 *I will give thanks to Thou, O Lord, my God, with all my heart, and will glorify Thy name forever"* (Ps. 86:8, 10-12).

Objective B: Instruction

A church is not only a worshiping community, it is a learning congregation. *They were continually devoting themselves to the apostles' teaching* (Acts 2:42). Interestingly, that's first on the list. Why? Because babies need food. True, they need love and tenderness and cleansing, but they cry for food. Verse 44 goes on to inform us, *Those who had believed were together.* If we read between the lines of this verse, we find that the early church had something worth listening to, something in which to believe—a body of truth to which those gathered were committed.

One of the marks of a healthy, growing church is the consistent, faithful instruction in the Word of God. Here are several benefits that grow out of regular teaching of the Word:

1. It gives substance to our faith.
2. It stabilizes us in times of testing.
3. It enables us to deal with the Bible correctly, so we can nourish ourselves with its meat.
4. It equips us to detect and confront error.
5. It makes us confident in our walk.
6. It calms our fears and conceals our superstitions.

Always keep in mind the primary purpose for our instruction: the glory of God. Knowledge is a wonderful thing, but knowledge alone can be dangerous.

1 *Now concerning things offered to idols: We know that we all have knowledge. Knowledge puffs up, but love edifies . . ..*

11 *And because of your knowledge shall the weak brother perish, for whom Christ died?*

12 *But when you thus sin against the brethren, and wound their weak conscience, you sin against Christ* (1 Cor. 8:1; 11-12).

When knowledge remains theoretical, it breeds indifference. When it isn't balanced by love and grace, it breeds intolerance. When it becomes an end in itself, it breeds idolatry.

Spiritual starvation

Famine is a grotesque and global reality. We've all seen heart-wrenching pictures of starving, emaciated children with their skinny legs and protruding bellies. But the prophet Amos describes another, more acute famine—a famine of the soul.

11 *"Behold, the days are coming," says the Lord God, that I will send a famine on the land, not a famine of bread, nor a thirst for water, but of hearing the words of the Lord.*

12 *They shall wander from sea to sea, and from north to east; they shall run to and fro, seeking the word of the Lord, but shall not find it.*

13 *In that day the fair virgins and strong young men shall faint from thirst"* (Amos 8:11-13).

That is the spiritual condition of most people in the world.

They are starving for truth. Their energies are wasted; their trust is waning, their hope is withered. When the bottom drops out, they don't know where to turn. When their lives are at a crossroad, they don't know which direction to take. Lost in a desert, they look desperately for an oasis of truth.

I thank God for Bible-study classes, for faithful men and women who study the Word of God to teach its life-changing truths, and for students who faithfully attend. As with the early church our congregations can be learning congregations.

Objective C: Fellowship

The fellowship ministry of the church is to connect the lost people of the world to Christ and the believers to each other. The focus of our lesson next week is on the latter—connecting believers to one another.

The Bible shows that the early church is a caring flock. This is revealed in Acts 2:44-45,

> 44 *Now all who believed were together, and had all things in common,*
> 45 *and sold their possessions and goods, and divided them among all, as anyone had need* (Acts 2:44-45).

The early church devoted itself to fellowship. The Greek word *koinonia*, with the root *koinos*, has the idea of something being held "in common." That is the thought of verse 44.

New Testament church members not only have things in common, they are together. They are not like a bunch of isolated marbles that make a lot of noise and scatter in all directions. They are like a cluster of grapes. When the winepress of persecution squeezes down on them, people in this close body of believers bleed together. Out of this painful, crushing experience springs the sweet wine of fellowship. We might define *fellowship* as an "expression of genuine Christianity, freely shared among God's members." Our final purpose of the church, "expression", grows out of fellowship.

Objective D: Expression

In the New Testament are two definite expressions of fellowship. The first is to connect people to Christ. We refer to this as *evangelism.*

> 46 *So continuing daily with one accord in the temple, and breaking bread from house to house, they ate their food with gladness and simplicity of heart,*
> 47 *praising God and having favor with all the people. And the Lord added to the church daily those who were being saved* (Acts 2:46-47).

In the early church that the Bible describes, clearly the quality of fellowship draws people into the church rather than drives them away. People go to the church because the gospel is taken into the streets to them.

> 1 *Now Peter and John went up together to the temple at the hour of prayer, the ninth hour.*
> 2 *And a certain man lame from his mother's womb was carried, whom they laid daily at the gate of the temple which is called Beautiful, to ask alms from those who entered the temple;*
> 3 *who, seeing Peter and John about to go into the temple, asked for alms.*
> 4 *And fixing his eyes on him, with John, Peter said, "Look at us."*
> 5 *So he gave them his attention, expecting to receive something from them.*

6 *Then Peter said, "Silver and gold I do not have, but what I do have I give you: In the name of Jesus Christ of Nazareth, rise up and walk."*

7 *And he took him by the right hand and lifted him up, and immediately his feet and ankle bones received strength.*

8 *So he, leaping up, stood and walked and entered the temple with them—walking, leaping, and praising God*

1 *Now as they spoke to the people, the priests, the captain of the temple, and the Sadducees came upon them,*

2 *being greatly disturbed that they taught the people and preached in Jesus the resurrection from the dead.*

3 *And they laid hands on them, and put them in custody until the next day, for it was already evening* (Acts 3:1-8; 4:1-3).

These are a few sample passages, because evangelism is the nature of the early church fellowship. The people cannot stop speaking about what Christ's resurrection has meant to their lives.

Evangelism in the New Testament

Here are some traits of evangelism in the New Testament:

1. It was never limited to the church facilities.
2. It was always initiated by the Christian. People did not go to church to find Christ; Christians took

Christ into the world to find people.

3. It was usually connected with another unrelated event or experience—i.e. a healing, an imprisonment, a conversation, a need which led naturally to the issue of who Jesus is.

4. People were not forced into it. Never once was an unsaved person manipulated, persecuted, and conformed with truth. They were not manipulated into believing. They were treated with dignity, with respect, and with intelligence.

Secondly, fellowship was the sharing of something with someone else or sharing in something with someone else.

The outgrowth of the first three purposes provides for the expression to effectively build the kingdom.

Service is our activity focused on building the kingdom. How do we serve God here and now? We serve God by serving people. We lay up treasure in heaven by investing in people who are going to heaven.

When the Crystal Palace Exhibition opened in 1851, people flocked to London's Hyde Park to behold the marvels. One of the greatest marvels back then was steam. Displayed there were steam plows, steam locomotives, steam organs, and even a steam cannon.

Of all the great exhibits that year, the first-prize winner was a steam invention with 7,000 parts. When it was turned on, its pulleys, whistles, bells, and gears made a lot of noise, but ironically, the contraption didn't do a thing! Seven-thousand moving parts making a lot of commotion, but the invention had no practical use.

Ministry is not simply activity; ministry is designed to accomplish the plan and principles of God. This is a study with a purpose. The depth of a church is determined by the quality of its worship and instruction. We can't give up on worship because we believe in instruction. Neither should we stop teaching because we love to worship. Rather, the qualities of each are what give a church strength, stability, and discernment.

The breadth of the church is determined by its commitment to fellowship and service. If we stop evangelism, we will become an exclusive clique instead of a caring church. If we don't reach out, we will become ingrown. When the church is accomplishing these four things, it will be contagious.

II. Four Mandates

God has given us four mandates as a church. We see these in 1 Thessalonians 2:1-13:

> 1 *For you yourselves know, brethren, that our coming to you was not in vain.*
>
> 2 *But even after we had suffered before and were spitefully treated at Philippi, as you know, we were bold in our God to speak to you the gospel of God in much conflict.*
>
> 3 *For our exhortation did not come from error or uncleanness, nor was it in deceit.*
>
> 4 *But as we have been approved by God to be entrusted with the gospel, even so we speak, not as pleasing men, but God who tests our hearts.*
>
> 5 *For neither at any time did we use flattering words, as you know, nor a cloak for covetousness—God is witness.*
>
> 6 *Nor did we seek glory from men, either from you or from others, when we might have made demands as apostles of Christ.*
>
> 7 *But we were gentle among you, just as a nursing*

mother cherishes her own children.

8 *So, affectionately longing for you, we were well pleased to impart to you not only the gospel of God, but also our own lives, because you had become dear to us.*

9 *For you remember, brethren, our labor and toil; for laboring night and day, that we might not be a burden to any of you, we preached to you the gospel of God.*

10 *You are witnesses, and God also, how devoutly and justly and blamelessly we behaved ourselves among you who believe;*

11 *as you know how we exhorted, and comforted, and charged every one of you, as a father does his own children,*

12 *that you would walk worthy of God who calls you into His own kingdom and glory.*

13 *For this reason we also thank God without ceasing, because when you received the word of God which you heard from us, you welcomed it not as the word of men, but as it is in truth, the word of God, which also effectively works in you who believe* (1 Thess. 2:1-13).

From this we see we are to—

1) Be biblical in content. The church is about the message, not the messenger. The church that remains biblical in content will become known as a place that tells the truth. It will be a place that establishes its convictions on the bedrock of God's voice of authority and not on the shifting sands of human opinion.

2) Be authentic in nature. Authenticity occurs when real people say real things about real issues with real feelings. How you stay real involves living what you are, telling the truth, and admitting your failures and weaknesses.

To be the best church member possible, ask yourself these questions:

- How real am I?
- Does an authentic life back up my words?
- Does an ulterior motive lurk behind my decisions and conversations?
- Do I seek my own glory and the praise of other people?
- Do I exploit my authority as a parent, partner, or professional?

3) Have a gracious attitude. The Bible shows that instead of being harsh and demanding, Paul is gentle and tolerant. Instead of sounding like an officer, he is like a tender, nursing mother. Instead of simply imparting only truth, he imparts his own life as well. Both Paul and the church at Thessalonica exhibit compassion, tact, and tenderness in their daily lives.

Ask yourself:

- How do I act with those who are struggling?
- Do those attitudes underlie my actions?

Carl Sandburg, describing Abraham Lincoln, called him *a man of steel and velvet.*

"Not often in the story of mankind does a man arrive on earth who is both steel and velvet, who is as hard as rock and as soft as drifting fog, who holds in his heart and mind the paradox of terrible storm and peace, unspeakable and perfect. While the lack of war wavered and broke and came again, as generals failed and campaigns were lost, he held enough forces together to raise new armies and supply them, until generals were found who made war as victorious has always been made, with terror, frightfulness, destruction, valor, and sacrifice past words of men to tell. In the mixed shame and blame of the immense wrongs of two crashing civilizations, often with nothing to say, he said nothing, slept not at all, and on occasions he was seen to weep in a way that made weeping appropriate, decent, majestic. That's a picture of a man who pursues God."

4) Be relevant in our approach. No such thing as the sacred and the secular exists. The way people conduct their business is no less sacred than the way they conduct their worship. Christ penetrates all of it. Jesus penetrates life from Wall Street to Main Street.

George McLeod wrote a poem entitled "Return the Cross to Golgotha" that helps put a lot of things in perspective. It helps to emphasize content rather than cosmetics, Christ rather than self, the gospel going beyond the church walls rather than simply being contained within them.

I simply argue that the cross be raised again
at the center of the market place
as well as on the steeple of the church,
I am recovering the claim that
Jesus was not crucified in a cathedral
between two candles:
But on a cross between two thieves;
on a town garbage heap;
at a crossroad of politics so cosmopolitan
that they had to write His title
in Hebrew and in Latin and in Greek . . .
And at the kind of place where cynics talk smut,
and thieves curse and soldiers gamble.

Because that is where He died,
and that is what He died about.
And that is where Christ's men ought to be,
and what Church people ought to be about.

If the contagious style occurs in our lives and in our church, what can we expect? We can expect that God will honor our efforts despite our weaknesses and imperfections. We can expect that we will model first-century Christlikeness in 21st-century time. We can expect that others will desire to join us in spite of our difficulties.

We want to exalt Christ and bless our mother, the church. The church is about people, not structures!

Some questions to consider:

1. Think about this earlier statement—"The (worship) experience is designed to equip you to feel clean and fresh—ready to face the challenges God has placed before you." Think about times when this has been a reality with you—that worship truly has left you feeling this way. What occurred in your worship experience to make this feeling happen in your life?

2. What keeps us from being able to seek God's face and genuinely worship Him when the bottom drops out of our lives?

3. What are some things that keep church members from being *together* as those in the early church were? What kinds of things keep us from acting as though we are separate marbles and more like clusters of grapes?

4. What do you think about the statement that in the early church, evangelism was never limited to church facilities?

Why is grasping this concept today so difficult for us? What are some ways that we can move beyond the idea that evangelism is something that happens only at church and only by church leaders such as the pastor?

5. What kinds of ulterior motives (mentioned in the earlier questions) could possibly be at play involving one's conversations or decisions at church?

6. Consider the previous statement, "The way people conduct their business is no less sacred than the way they conduct their worship." Think about your life. Does Christ penetrate your business dealings? If so, how? If not, what could you do to make this statement applicable to you?

7. Think about your local church body. What about your church would cause someone to want to join you despite knowing that your church is not perfect and that you, as its members, are human beings with the normal problems of life?

8. Early converts are described as eating and working with the same spirit of exultant joy with which they prayed and broke bread. Does this description apply to you? Do you carry into your workplace the joy of living that you might experience within the walls of the church? Could someone who observes you on the job want to know more about how he or she could adapt the kind of joy you exude? Could your positive attitude in time of workplace anxiety provide a springboard for you to share about hope in Christ? Could it give you a launching pad for you to invite someone to attend worship with you?

9. These converts seemed to spend a goodly portion of time each day in social interaction. This concept may seem very foreign to those of us who live frenetic lives in Western society and who often rely on instant electronic communication such as emails and blogs to convey our innermost thoughts. We may wonder how these had time to fellowship so

freely? With today's time constraints, how could we do a better job of this social aspect that the early believers in this close-knit church seem to exhibit?

10. These converts seem not to be able to stop speaking about what they have seen and heard—what Christ's resurrection means to them personally. How does this apply to you? Do you give credit where credit is due? Do you interject into your casual conversations with others your awareness of God as the source of all your blessings? Do you communicate that awareness to others?

11. How transparent are we in our churches about our personal struggles and challenges as well as triumphs? Are we still more of a "museum for saints" rather than a "hospital for sinners"? Do we still try to put our "best foot forward" rather than being honest about what's really going on in our lives? Looking too "goody-goody" may turn off struggling seekers who wonder whether the church has anything to offer them. How much does "image" matter when we gather as a body of believers?

12. Is our concept of "church-growth" simply numerical? The early church grew in the sense of learning, of caring fellowship, and worshiping—by being faithful to God and to each other. Are we intentional in focusing on those aspects of growth as well as in our outreach efforts? What could you do personally to be sure your church excels in those three regards to be a successful, ongoing body of believers?

13. The Scripture notes that "the Lord added" to the early church. This reminds us that God's calling is what is instrumental in bringing people to Christ. How can we balance our awareness of this with our contemporary programs and strategies for evangelism?

Lesson #1

Be Supportive of One Another

1 Corinthians 12:25

Tom Sawyer said, "Church ain't shucks to the circus!" Many people—perhaps a majority in our world today—might share in his uninformed opinion. However, if Tom Sawyer had any idea at all about how splendid the church really is, he never would have made that remark.

By contrast, Jesus speaks of the church in a totally positive light. The Bible says He calls it "*my church.*" The Bible pictures the church as the Bride of Christ. Jesus never speaks of "my country" or "my school," or "my government", yet He refers to "*my church*" with great affection and unswerving loyalty.

We form the Body of Christ. Paul says we are . . . *members one of another* (Rom. 12:5). Just as a physical body has many parts—such as eyes, ears, hands, feet—a spiritual body also has many parts. Many believers don't understand the "body life" that God wants them to enjoy. This is why many today wouldn't consider being a church member to be a highlight of their resumés. This might not be the case, however, if these believers were participating in a church that was functioning as God designed it (as the introduction describes.)

How do you become part of the body?

The simple answer is:

1. I become part of the family of Christ by committing my life to Jesus Christ as Lord.

2. I become part of the congregational family by committing my life to people of like faith who are brothers and sisters in the Lord.

The prerequisite to being part of the church is to be born into God's family. You don't just join a church as you would a country club but with smaller dues. Since people can't get anywhere close to becoming divine, God has to make the transition. This is what Bethlehem is all about. The Bible says that to enter our experience fully, Jesus enters this world as a baby. He lives a sinless and perfect life. If humanity is going to be brought into the Godhead, that humanity has to undergo every temptation without even once succumbing to sin. Just one sin, however slight and seemingly insignificant, would have brought the entire project to terminal failure.

Jesus then has to die on the cross to atone for our sin. To redeem humanity from the curse, justice requires that a sinless being would have to take on Himself all the sins of the world—past, present, and future. In the judicial system of God, a lamb without blemish is required. The sin-bearer of the world has to be a person without sin.

Jesus has to be raised from the dead, because if death had the final word, then no more union with God the Father could occur. Since all that Jesus has done on the earth is done with a dependency on the Father and with a heart to please the Father, the Father would have to approve and glorify the resurrected life of Jesus before the next step could occur.

The next spot, of which John 7:39 speaks, is the separating of the Holy Spirit into the perfect life of Jesus that has been glorified by the Father. Romans 8:2 speaks of the *Spirit of life in Christ Jesus*. What this refers to is the fact that the Holy Spirit cocooned Himself into what had never existed before—a life that was fully human and fully divine and also fully tested and fully glorified. With all this having been accomplished, this unique life of God, through God's divine nature, brings life to the dead soul of man separated from God because of sin. Only then could the believer be placed by the Holy Spirit into the body of Christ.

Pentecost marks the beginning of the Holy Spirit's indwelling of believers on a permanent basis. A person can no more make himself or herself part of God's Kingdom than a product of the vegetable kingdom could make itself part of the animal kingdom.

The Greek word for church is *ecclesia,* from which we get our word *ecclesiastical.* The literal meaning is to "be called out." Picture, if you will, Jesus speaking the universe into existence or Jesus standing at dead Lazarus' tomb and saying to his dead body, "Come." Jesus calls him out. In the same way Jesus calls out those whose souls are dead and brings them into the Kingdom of God. We have been called from darkness to light, from bondage to freedom, from sin to righteousness, and from self to the Savior.

In the Bible the word *Christian* is given to believers in Antioch; it is not used as a compliment. The people are saying, "You are like Christ." But from a heavenly perspective they are complimenting the believers. *Christ* means "anointed one"; therefore, a Christian is a bearer of the anointing. The anointing is a sweetness and straightness, supernatural in character, which will touch the spirit, illumine the mind, stir the soul, persuade the will, and heal the body. Out of this anointing we are able to evangelize the world and edify fellow believers.

This week and throughout the 12 weeks that follow, we will study the commands of the "one-another"s through the anointing of God. How exciting to be a member of a church! To be a member of this body is to have the very nature of Jesus. Just think of that—being a church member means you have Jesus' nature. Does this realization elevate your estimation of your church membership? Being part of a church is to be a bearer of his yoke-bearing anointing. It is to have an influence that will ripple all the way to the shores of eternity.

How do members function?

Believers grow in fellowship with Jesus and with one another. Throughout this week and the remaining 12 weeks we will get a greater insight into what it means to fellowship one with another.

I. As believers we are supportive to one another.

A. We care for one another.

> 25 . . . *that there should be no schism in the body, but that the members should have the same care for one another* (1 Cor. 12:25).

1. The church meets the needs of other believers. According to the Bible story, people in the first-century church in Jerusalem take on themselves the task of meeting the physical needs of others. At the time of Pentecost, people are in Jerusalem from all over the world. When the Holy Spirit gives birth to the church, thousands of people believe in Christ. These people stay there for a period of time before they return to their homes. Providing for them presents a crisis.

2. The church has the idea of being a Good Samaritan as Luke 10 describes. The man in this passage finds himself in several crises—left, robbed, wounded, and half-dead. Religion and legalism pass him by, but a person with the character of God stops to make a difference.

3. This type of heart is not always found in the church. Paul says in Philippians 2:20, *I have no man . . . who will care for me*. So many Christians have their own agendas. Being intentionally blind to the needs of fellow believers is easy. We are less and less moved with compassion for hurting people, both within and without the church. Let's not leave pastoral care solely to the pastors; it is the ministry of all of us.

B. We comfort one another.

First Thessalonians 4:18 says, *Therefore comfort one another with these words*. How do we give comfort? We are able to comfort believers with what we have learned about how God has comforted us. Most of our best ministry springs out of our own past hurts. 2 Corinthians 1:3 says, *Blessed be the God and Father of our Lord Jesus Christ, the Father of mercies and God of all comfort* . . . (2 Cor. 1:3). We don't have all the answers; religious platitudes are at best insulting. The Bible says we have the burden of being considerate of others' fears and feelings. We are much more likely to think that the fears of others are unnecessary but that our own fears are real. As I allow God to work in my life, I become more and more understanding, especially if I have experienced some similar painful experience in my own life. I am able to go beyond sympathy to empathy.

Of course the greatest comfort I can give to people is to introduce them to the Lord Jesus. Jesus says of the believer, "*Blessed are they that mourn; for they shall be comforted*" (Matt. 5:4).

Comforted by who? By God! Having introduced them to Jesus and confirming they are in a relationship with Christ, we can help them learn to depend on the sustaining grace of God.

C. We are to encourage one another.

Not a single person in the world exists who does not need encouragement. We possess many virtues to help us accomplish this command, but nothing happens until we become intentional. Everyone needs to be recognized; everyone needs to be rewarded. As believers we build up each other when we do this.

II. As believers we are to confront one another.

The truth is that many of our brothers and sisters in Christ either are on the verge or in the midst of sin. Paul tells the Roman Christians that they are to admonish one another (Rom. 15:14). That means to sound a warning or give strong advice.

In other words, we are to teach the truth in love. In later lessons we will be more specific, but we admonish one another as we:

- Confess to one another.
- Make peace with one another.
- Teach one another.

Also, we are to be of sound mind one to another. In Acts 20 Paul reminds believers that he constantly admonishes them with tears. If we care, we will be willing to confront. Only truth can bring unity in the church; our Lord wants us united. We do this without speaking evil of each other but rather to stir up one another for the cause of Christ.

Some questions to consider:

1. The opening paragraph of our lesson refers to the church as *splendid*. Do you agree with that description? (We're of course not talking about the quality of one's physical church

structure.) Does the Body of Christ itself, to you, feel "splendid"? Why or why not? For you personally, what would the church have to be like to make it be "splendid" in your estimation?

2. Why do you believe the heart of the Good Samaritan is not always found among church people? Why do you believe that people's own agendas get in the way of meeting the needs of others in the body? What could you do personally to be sure that you have a compassionate heart that puts feet to your compassion?

3. Do you believe that Christians are willing to "support" others in the church in certain prescribed ways but not in others? Helping someone at the time of illness or bereavement usually occurs naturally for the church, but what about a person who loses a job? goes to jail? has some type of moral failing? has a child with an unplanned pregnancy? is the victim of rumor or gossip? What can you personally do to "think outside the box" when you are confronted with someone's critical emotional need?

4. Describe some effective ways you have found to render comfort to someone else. Does comfort always involve saying "the right words"? When can silence in the presence of someone needing support be the most godly means of comfort you can offer?

5. How did you react when you read the statement, "We possess many virtues to help us accomplish (encouraging each other), but nothing happens until we become intentional"? Did you agree or disagree? What keeps us from affirming each other? If verbal affirmation is not your "love language", yet you recognize that many others need verbal pats on the back, in what ways can you stretch yourself to be more verbally affirming?

6. How do you feel when, in times of trouble, you realize

that the very comfort you can receive springs directly from the throneroom of God Himself and that He is ready and available to meet your needs? How readily do you remind others of God's sufficiency?

7. Since it clearly is a scriptural precept, why does the thought of holding each other accountable or sounding an alarm to another who is in sin intimidate us? How can admonishing each other be done in love and in a way that edifies instead of alienates?

Lesson #2

Love One Another

John 13:34-35

For you and me as God's people to make an impact on this world in which we live is vitally important! This begins with a right relationship with God and a right relationship with each other. One of the biggest misunderstandings we have about the Christian life is thinking that we can get along with God and not get along with each other. But that is a lie; you can't love God if you hate your brother or sister. We are studying the "one-another" statements in the New Testament because they teach us practical ways to love one another.

If you check your concordance and your New Testament, you will find 12 different references that contain these words, "*Love one another*." Additionally, we find many other references in the Bible about Christian love, but today I want to focus on the statements that tell us to "*Love one another*."

The story is told of a Catholic priest who had been assigned to a new parish. Wanting to know what his people were really like, he decided to go, without being announced, to the new town earlier than he was expected. On arrival he dressed as a beggar and went to the marketplace. There he studied his people as they went about their day-to-day business.

One day he found himself talking to a prim, proper woman who was well-schooled in biblical knowledge. The conversation soon turned to religion. "How many commandments are in

Scripture?" she asked. The beggar replied, "Eleven." Horrified at such ignorance she said, "Obviously you know nothing about God at all!" She then turned and walked away.

The next Sunday this not-so-dear woman arrived at church only to discover that the beggar she had encountered was, in actuality, the new priest. What stunned her even more was the message he presented. The message was entitled, "The Eleventh Commandment." The priest's text was from the words of our Blessed Lord in the Upper Room,

> 34 "*A new commandment I give to you, that you love one another; as I have loved you, that you also love one another.*
>
> 35 *By this all will know that you are My disciples, if you have love for one another*" (John 13:34-35).

Somehow what the woman missed, not only in her scholarship of Scripture but also in her life, was the very badge of Christianity: love for fellow believers.

Actually, this command is given many times in the Bible—1 Thessalonians 4:9, John 14:2, and Romans 13:8. First John 5:1 says, *Everyone who loves him who begot also loves him who's begotten of him.* This means that if we love the Lord, the One who enabled our "born-again" experience, then we're going to love others who, like ourselves, also are born again. One day Jesus stood before a crowd and asked, "*Who is my mother? Who are my brothers?*" Then answering His own question, He proceeded to say, "*Whoever does the will of My Father in Heaven is my brother and my sister and my mother*" (Matt. 12:50). Notice he's not speaking of His Father, for no human being can substitute for that relationship. But even for us, spiritual kinship can be stronger and dearer than can flesh-and-blood kinship, just as it was for Jesus. This increase of intimacy happens, not because biological families are intentionally minimized. Members of a family which isn't Christian, or perhaps isn't pursuing with much desire what God has for them, just can't share in those experiences that a growing Christian family holds dear.

What exactly constitutes the kind of love that only growing Christians can share? Whenever we talk about love, it seems like a "mushy, never, never-land" description. Let's look at this love from a biblical perspective.

I. God's command

Jesus says this is *a new commandment*. In John 15:12 He says, " *This is My commandment, that you love one another as I have loved you.*" In John 15:15 he repeats this command. Is that right for God to make such a demand? Another question: Can a young man command a young woman who is uninterested in Him to love him? Of course not! Then how can God command us to *love one another*?

Understand that Christian love is not an emotional feeling that we manufacture. Christian love means this: We treat each other the way God treats us. Christian love is not a matter of feeling; it's a matter of willing. "*God so loved . . . that He gave* . . .." (John 3:16). God's love is not a sentimental feeling. God's love expresses itself in action. Christian love is an act of the will; we will to treat each other the way God treats us.

> 4 *Love suffers long and is kind; love does not envy; love does not parade itself, is not puffed up;*
> 5 *does not behave rudely, does not seek its own, is not provoked, thinks no evil;*
> 6 *does not rejoice in iniquity, but rejoices in the truth;*
> 7 *bears all things, believes all things, hopes all things, endures all things* (1 Cor. 13:4-7).

This passage denotes the character of God's love for us and describes what love does and doesn't do. The whole passage is void of any statement about rapturous feelings that love does produce. Instead, it focuses on the behaviors of love. We find at least two reasons for this.

> 1) Feelings always follow behavior. If a person, in obedience to the Lord, will simply do what God says to do, the feelings of love will later emerge.
>
> 2) Feelings don't always last. You may have heard about the guy who said, "Yesterday I loved my wife so much I could have eaten her up. Today I wish I had."

Question: How does God treat us? God forgives us, so we forgive each other. God is kind to us, so we are kind to each other. God receives us, and so we receive each other. We may not have the same personalities, or we might not even have the same interests, but we willingly and deliberately treat each other the way God treats us. That is what loving one another means.

The interesting thing is this: the more we deliberately will to *love one another*, the more our feelings begin to change. Lo and behold, we even start to like one another.

You might not want to spend a week of vacation with some Christians, but you can still treat them the way God treats you. As we *love one another* more and more, we learn to like one another. We can get along with one another to the glory of God. So the first reason we should *love one another* is because God commands it. Jesus Christ has every right to command us because He reveals His love to us. He says, "*Greater love hath no man than this, that a man lay down his life for his friends*" (John 15:13). But the Scriptures tell us that He lays down His life for His enemies.

8 *But God demonstrates His own love toward us, in that while we were still sinners, Christ died for us.*

10 *For if when we were enemies we were reconciled to God through the death of His Son, much more, having been reconciled, we shall be saved by His life* (Rom. 5:8; 10).

By His life and by His death, He gives us the perfect example of love.

II. God's law

Romans 13:8 repeats this commandment to *love one another*. In this chapter Paul discusses our relationship to government and to the law. "*Owe no man anything, but to love one another; for he that loveth another hath fulfilled the law.*" The Old Testament Jews had many laws to keep—laws that governed the land, laws concerning his relationship to property and his neighbor, laws about the tabernacle and the sacrifices. But Paul says that, for the New Testament Christian, one command takes care of all the regulations. If I love you, I'm not going to try and kill you; if I love you, I'm not going to steal from you; if I love you, I'm not going to bear false witness against you.

The moral law of God still stands. The righteousness of God's law still is required. However, we do not obey the law from external fear; we obey the law from internal love. It is not compulsion on the outside; it is compassion on the inside. We *love one another*; this love takes care of all the commandments that God gave in the law about our relationships.

Love is not a substitute for the law for me to say, "I love you, and that takes care of it!" It does not really take care of it. Love helps us fulfill the law. *Love* is a verb—an action word. Love is the motivation for obedience.

III. God's teaching

In 1 Thessalonians 3:12 we find another reference to *love one another*. Paul prays for the church.

> 12 *And may the Lord make you increase and abound in love to one another and to all, just as we do to you* . . . (1 Thess. 3:12).

> 9 *But concerning brotherly love you have no need that I should write to you, for you yourselves are taught by God to love one another* . . . (1 Thess. 4:9).

God the Father teaches us to *love one another* by giving His Son. God the Son teaches us to *love one another* by giving His life. God the Holy Spirit who lives within us teaches us to love one another.

> 5 *Now hope does not disappoint, because the love of God has been poured out in our hearts by the Holy Spirit who was given to us* (Rom. 5:5).

As previously mentioned the greatest evidence of Christian discipleship is love (John 13:35). What is the evidence that one is a true disciple? Carrying a Bible? Anyone can carry a Bible. Singing a praise song? Anyone can sing a song. Going to church? Anyone can do that also. What identifies a true disciple of Jesus Christ? True disciples *love one another.*

IV. God's nature

In 1 Peter 1:22-23, the apostle says that we should *love one another* because this is a part of our new birth. He says, *Seeing ye have purified your souls in obeying the truth through the*

Spirit unto unfeigned love as the brethren, see that ye love one another with a pure heart fervently, being born again. The new nature of God within us gives us the power to love.

My old nature is not very loving of anyone but myself; it loves the things that are wrong. Paul writes in Titus 3:3 that once we were hateful and hating one another. But when you are born again and you receive that wonderful new nature of God, love moves in. Do you know why? *God is love . . .* (1 John 4:8). Since God is love and God is my Heavenly Father, then I share my Father's nature. So I should love; I should share love.

First Peter 1:22 states that this love should be *unfeigned*. That means sincere, not artificial. Some people gush all over us because they want us to think that they love us, but it is only so much talk. *Unfeigned* love means sincere love, fervent love, *. . . with a pure heart fervently* (v. 22). That *pure heart* is important. If my heart is not pure, this means sin is in my heart. If sin is in my heart, I really cannot love you, because sin is basically selfishness. If fervent love is to emerge from my heart, my heart has to be pure.

Here then are three characteristics of Christian love: *Unfeigned* (sincere), *pure*, and *fervent*. The word *fervent* describes the striving of an athlete. The kind of energy that an athlete puts into winning the game, we should put into loving each other. I wonder if we are as energetic about our love as we are about our sports involvements?

In 1 John 3 are five verses that say, *Love one another*. We read in 1 John 3:11, *For this is the message that you heard from the beginning, that we should love one another.* This statement relates to verse 10, *If we are the children of God, we are going to love one another.* And in 1 John 3:23, *And this is the commandment, that we should believe on the name of His Son Jesus Christ, and love one another, as He gave us commandments.* And in 1 John 4:7-8, *Beloved, let us love one another. For love is of God; and everyone that loveth is born of God, and knoweth God. He that loveth not knoweth not God; for God is love.*

God commands us to love. Then He puts within us His own nature to enable us to love each other. The new birth creates within us a desire to love God and to love others. First John 4:11 states, *Beloved, if God so loved us, we ought also to love one another. No man hath seen God at any time. If we love one another, God dwelleth in us, and His love is perfected in us.* That is an interesting statement. People can't see God, but they can see God's children. And if God's children are loving each other, then the world will know how wonderful knowing God is. The tragedy is that often the world looks at God's people and cannot see that they *love one another.*

I fear sometimes the world looks at us and says, "Look how they disagree with each other—how they fight with each other."

All these passages refer to the same wonderful privilege—the privilege we have of loving one another. But all of this has to be practiced. If we *love one another*, we will treat each other the way God treats us. This means forgiving one another, being kind to one another, and seeking to build up one another. As we study the "one-another" statements, we will see how practical Christian love can be.

The practice of love is not just what we do for one another, it's what we don't do to one another. For example, the character of Christian love *does not envy*. We are not jealous of one another. What a monster envy is! What damage it does in God's family! To love each other is not to be jealous of what a person is or has but to find pleasure in our loved ones' good success. We move the focus from ourselves to others. Christian love is not being arrogant or behaving rudely; simply put, *it does not seek its own.* That means our lives are not "thin-skinned"; we do not allow ourselves to be set off by some minor irritation. Literally our love is *not provoked.* We say, "It's not about me." In the midst of my Christian relationships I often recite this question, "Will this matter one second inside of eternity?" If the answer is *no*, it's not really a big deal.

Paul reminds us that the character of God's love *thinks no evil.* What a challenge in a culture that looks for the worst instead of the best in other people. How sad that Christians not only look for the worst in their brothers and sisters, they rejoice in their iniquities. We delight in the fall of others, but that really should break our hearts. We become absorbed in some juicy scandal, especially when it involves church leadership.

The character of Christian love *believes all things.* Therefore, it rejoices in truth even if truth is painful, because it is truth that sets us free. Whatever the sin, whatever the suffering, true love shoulders the burden and brings it all to God. This burden-bearing involves teaming up against sin, self, and Satan with an intent to diminish the influence of each. We often hear, "love is blind," but love is far from blind; it sees what God sees and believes with God that all things are possible. God's grace can empower everyone to live out God's purposes and plans. Because love has hope woven into its fiber, it refuses to give up or give out. Perfect love casts out fear and gives us courage to go forward and go together.

Christian love is produced by the Spirit of Christ. The Holy Spirit produces His fruit in us. The secret of fruit-bearing is abiding in Christ. When a Christian (the branch) is connected to the Vine (Christ), His life flows through us. The result is the Fruit of the Spirit being produced as we love with Christ's love.

Some questions to consider:

1. More than anything else, loving one another reveals whether we are truly Christians. Neither the church we attend

nor the doctrines we believe indicate this. How we show our love for each other is what demonstrates our Christianity. In what ways does Jesus make this clear in John 13:35?

2. When Jesus makes this statement in John 13:35, He gives the world the right to judge us by our love. What are requirements for loving one another as the Bible teaches?

3. Think of a personal experience of intimacy with a Christian brother or sister that may exceed one that you have with a family member. Why is this possible?

4. Think of a time in which you actually willed yourself to love someone you didn't like. What happened?

5. If the mark of a true disciple is his or her love for others, how would you measure up in this kind of evaluation? By observing you, would an observer immediately say of you, "Look how much he or she follows Christ"? If the answer is *no,* what would be necessary for you to improve in this area?

6. Do you ever "gush all over" someone, as the lesson describes, but yet not really love the person? In other words, are you a hypocrite? If the answer is *yes*, what would be necessary for you to do better in this area?

7. How could you be more energetic in your love for others? How could you be as enthusiastic about showing love for others as you are in cheering in a sports game?

8. What about the lesson's statement, "I fear sometimes the world looks at us (believers) and says, 'Look how they disagree with each other; look at how they argue.'" What can you personally do to be sure the proper image is portrayed?

9. The lesson speaks of the true privilege we have of loving each other. Do you really consider this to be a privilege? What could you change about your life so that you truly regard the act of extending Christian love a privilege and not a curse?

Lesson #3

Wash One Another's Feet
John 13:1-17

Caring Christians love one another. This love is not a feeling they manufacture. God puts this love within their hearts. It is the work of the Holy Spirit as they yield to Him.

But loving one another is a very practical thing. It is not a matter of words only; it is a matter of deeds. When you say to someone, "I love you," that's one thing, but proving it by your actions is quite something else. This is why we are studying the "one-another" statements in the New Testament. One evidence of Christian love is our willingness to wash one another's feet.

Our text tells us what Jesus did, what Jesus is now doing, and what Jesus wants us to do.

> 1 *Now before the Feast of the Passover, when Jesus knew that His hour had come that He should depart from this world to the Father, having loved His own who were in the world, He loved them to the end.*
>
> 2 *And supper being ended, the devil having already put it into the heart of Judas Iscariot, Simon's son, to betray Him,*
>
> 3 *Jesus, knowing that the Father had given all things into His hands, and that He had come from God and was going to God,*
>
> 4 *rose from supper and laid aside His garments, took a towel and girded Himself.*

5 *After that, He poured water into a basin and began to wash the disciples' feet, and to wipe them with the towel with which He was girded.*

6 *Then He came to Simon Peter. And Peter said to Him, "Lord, are You washing my feet?"*

7 *Jesus answered and said to him, "What I am doing you do not understand now, but you will know after this."*

8 *Peter said to Him, "You shall never wash my feet!" Jesus answered him, "If I do not wash you, you have no part with Me."*

9 *Simon Peter said to Him, "Lord, not my feet only, but also my hands and my head!"*

10 *Jesus said to him, "He who is bathed needs only to wash his feet, but is completely clean; and you are clean, but not all of you."*

11 *For He knew who would betray Him; therefore He said, "You are not all clean."*

12 *So when He had washed their feet, taken His garments, and sat down again, He said to them, "Do you know what I have done to you?*

13 *You call Me Teacher and Lord, and you say well, for so I am.*

14 *If I then, your Lord and Teacher, have washed your feet, you also ought to wash one another's feet.*

15 *For I have given you an example, that you should do as I have done to you.*

16 *Most assuredly, I say to you, a servant is not greater than his master; nor is he who is sent greater than he who sent him.*

17 *If you know these things, blessed are you if you do them*" (John 13:1-17).

What Jesus does

Jesus humbles Himself. This is beautifully illustrated in Philippians 2:5-8,

> 5 *Let this mind be in you which was also in Christ Jesus,*
> 6 *who, being in the form of God, did not consider it robbery to be equal with God,*
> 7 *but made Himself of no reputation, taking the form of a bondservant, and coming in the likeness of men.*
> 8 *And being found in appearance as a man, He humbled Himself and became obedient to the point of death, even the death of the cross* (Phil. 2:5-8).

In Scripture Jesus is seen as the suffering servant. The Bible says God's thoughts are not our thoughts and His ways are beyond our finding out. The concept of the greater serving the lesser does not make sense in our minds, but this is the character of God and an example to us.

This event shocks the disciples. Peter becomes quite indignant about this humility. He does not want his Lord acting as though He is a servant. The reason Peter doesn't want this is because he knows that if he were the one in charge with power and glory, he would do no such thing. The disciples are concerned about who will have the highest place—and not the lowest—in the kingdom. The mother of James and John already has approached Jesus secretly about giving favor to her sons when Jesus enters into His glory. They are into thrones, but Jesus is into towels. In the midst of selfish ambitions Jesus teaches a kingdom principle: The greatest in God's kingdom is the servant. In our culture we are always ready to fight for the throne but rarely for the towel.

Because of this, the church is filled with half-empty people. We want fashion but have no passion; we are interested but not inspired; we have great abilities but seldom are available. We fail to see the way up is down!

> 42 *But Jesus called them to Himself and said to them, "You know that those who are considered rulers over the Gentiles lord it over them, and their great ones exercise authority over them.*
> 43 *Yet it shall not be so among you; but whoever desires to become great among you shall be your servant.*
> 44 *And whoever of you desires to be first shall be slave of all.*
> 45 *For even the Son of Man did not come to be served, but to serve, and to give His life a ransom for many"* (Mark 10:42-45).

What a revolutionary principle! Not how many can I boss, but how many can I serve? How different the average church would be if we would get this principle—a vision for serving! Famed evangelist D.L. Moody said, "I would rather wake up a slumbering church than a slumbering world . . . the man who does the most good in the world is not the man who works himself, but the man who sets others to work."

What Jesus does now

What is He doing now? Keeping His own people clean. In verse 10 we see an important distinction between being washed all over (bathed) and simply having your feet washed. Today we don't worry much about the problem of soiled feet, but back in

Jesus' day people did. Many people did not wear shoes; those who did wore simple sandals. The streets were not paved; people had dirty feet. When a guest arrived at your home, the person would remove his sandals at the door. Someone—the host or a servant—would wash the guest's feet. This was an important custom and the heart of hospitality.

When you were born again, you were washed all over. But as Christians walking through this world, our feet get dirty. We sin; we walk in the flesh rather than in the Spirit. Positionally we are in Christ and eternally secure, but practically sin hinders our fellowship with Christ and with each other. Salvation is a once-and-for-all washing, but believers need moment-by-moment cleansing. At salvation, through spiritual birth we are justified. Through daily cleansing we are sanctified; in God's heaven we will be glorified. We can safely say, "I am saved from sin's penalty; I am being saved from sin's power; one day I will be saved from sin's presence." In our lives, while we are positionally all God wants us to be, we are in the practice of being conformed into His image.

First John 1:9 says, *If we confess our sins, He is faithful and just to forgive us our sins and to cleanse us from all unrighteousness.* That verse refers to believers. A Christian does not have more than one spiritual birth, but we must experience many spiritual cleansings.

What Jesus wants us to do

Jesus wants us to follow His servant example. Verse 15 says, "*I have given you an example, that you should do as I have done unto you.*" Notice He does not say, "*Do what I have done,*" but "*Do as I have done.*" Some churches practice washing the saints' feet as an ordinance of the gospel. This is not an ordinance, but doing the act is not wrong. Many blessings emerge from it. Jesus, however, is not focusing on an act but rather on an attitude. How wonderful if in doing an act alone we could please God! No, pleasing God involves much more than an act. So what does this attitude of washing one another's feet mean exactly? It means to have a humble attitude. We are to humble ourselves before one another, to minister to one another, and to take the place of a servant. Occasionally the host, as an honor, will wash guests' feet, but usually servants do this. Our Blessed Lord is the host at the Last Supper. But He also is God! Can you imagine God bowing before sinful people and washing their feet? He gives us an example of how Christian love works: an example of humility, an example of service, an example of putting others on a higher level than one's self.

This touches us where it really hurts! We live in a world that asks, "How high are you? What is your position?" Our Lord asks, "How low are you? Are you washing others' feet?"

The disciples, as you know, often argue over who is or will be the greatest. On a couple of occasions in the Gospels, our Lord Jesus rebukes them. We still have this problem today. When you read some magazines and some press releases, you find people fighting over who is the greatest, who has the greatest church, who is the greatest preacher. Our Lord says the important thing is to be the greatest servant.

Something in human nature does not want to get down before anyone else and be a servant, yet Jesus tells us that the happiest life is the life of service.

Jesus has all things placed in His hands. Out of all the things on which He might have focused, He focuses on the towel. This is the secret of humility. Humility occurs when we realize God has given us everything. We don't have to pretend, we don't have to act as though we are important, we don't have to tell people how big we are—we have everything (1 Cor. 3:21).

Everything has been put into our hands through Jesus Christ. We don't need to fight for anything; we don't have to struggle for anything. It is all ours. We possess all things through Christ.

When you realize this great truth, you can reach out, take up a towel, and serve other people. If Jesus Christ, the very Son of God, can do this, we can do it as well. He does it for us; we can follow His example and do this for others.

What does *washing others' feet* mean in practicality? It means being a blessing to them. It means helping them keep clean. It means refreshing them. In his Epistles the Apostle Paul often writes about people who have refreshed him. In 1 Corinthians 16:17-18, he writes about the saints who have refreshed him. In glowing terms He talks about people because they have refreshed him in the things of the Lord.

Have you refreshed anyone? When you are with people, does the life of God flow through you so that you refresh them? Or do you dry people out? Do you bore people spiritually?

The Gospel of John often uses the term *water*. Jesus tells the woman at the well He will put within her a well of living water. We ask the obvious question, "Where does that water flow?"

> 37 *On the last day, that great day of the feast, Jesus stood and cried out, saying, "If anyone thirsts, let him come to Me and drink.*
>
> 38 *He who believes in Me, as the Scripture has said, out of his heart will flow rivers of living water."*
>
> 39 *But this He spoke concerning the Spirit, whom those believing in Him would receive; for the Holy Spirit was not yet given, because Jesus was not yet glorified* (John 7:37-39).

The well of living water that refreshes me on the inside becomes a river of living water to flow out and to touch others' lives and to refresh them.

Most people have a difficult time serving other people. They struggle in doing anything for anyone else. Others seem to exist just to serve others. Our Lord said that if we want to experience holiness and want to experience happiness, then we are to practice humility. Where humbleness of heart exists, so does holiness of life. When you combine humility and holiness, you have happiness.

In the following verse, who do you think is happier, Mary or Martha?

> 40 *But Martha was distracted with much serving, and she approached Him and said, "Lord, do You not care that my sister has left me to serve alone? Therefore tell her to help me"* (Luke 10:40).

Martha's question to the Lord is, "Don't you even care I am working so diligently?" The attitude is, "You and Mary are having a great time but at whose expense? I'm in here slaving away for you two! This isn't fair!"

I wish I could say I have not been where Martha is in this circumstance. I have prayed, "God use me", and then felt used by people and became upset. I want to say, as Martha does, "Jesus, can't you see what's going on?; I'm being used!" The Holy Spirit had to remind me that I needed to make up my mind. Do I want to be used or not? Serving often feels like being used. The servant has no glamour. Our thoughts might be, "Oh, if God could only see what is going on", in terms of what we perceive as the unfairness of it all. That's what Martha seems to be thinking.

In *The Complete Green Letters,* Miles Stanford writes, "The majority of active members in our sound churches today are primarily doers. Their chief concern is to work for the Lord. But, service being the emphasis of their life, they are for the most part motivated by self. We must all learn, sooner or later, that the result of every form of self-effort is nothing but a barren waste, a spiritual death valley. Our growth is bound to falter and dry up when service is predominant in our life, especially in the formative years."

Martha is busy doing the Lord's work but is void of a servant's heart. We really only serve God in this world when we willingly serve people. We lay up treasure in heaven by investing in people who are going to heaven.

Jesus says, "*If anyone serves Me, let him follow Me . . ..*" (John 12:26) Where is Jesus going when He makes this statement? Jesus is on His way to the cross to die for our sins. He is going to a place of personal sacrifice so painful, to a trial so demanding, to a trust so complete, that no room for self-life exists. The cross is the destination for all who would follow Jesus and for all who would serve in the way He wants us to serve.

General William Booth, the founder of the Salvation Army, and a man who had been filled with the Holy Spirit, was asked the secret of his success. He replied, "I will tell you the secret, God has had all there was of me. There have been many men with greater brains than I, but from the day that I got the poor in London on my heart, and a vision of what Christ could do for them, I made up my mind that God should have all there was of William Booth. And if there is anything of power in my work, it is because God has had all the love of my heart, and all the power of my will, and all the influence of my life."

This is exactly what Paul talks about in Ephesians 6:6, *As bondservants of Christ, doing the will of God from the heart.* Isn't this a great expression of his inward desire? It doesn't represent an "Ah-gee, do I have to?" spirit but a true desire from a humble heart within.

So the next time we have the opportunity, let's serve others. The next time we have the opportunity, let's refresh others. Let's wash their feet spiritually. You may say, "Well, that means being a servant." That's right. Being a servant in the will of God is a thrilling, wonderful thing! I know being a servant is not easy. We have to pray and ask the Holy Spirit to help us. We are prone to defend ourselves and to want everyone to serve us. But how wonderful life can be when we experience the humility, happiness, and holiness of a life that is totally yielded to Christ—a life of serving others, of washing one another's feet.

Some questions to consider:

1. Through what ministries are you currently serving Christ?

2. List some of the great victories you have experienced on a personal level because you were willing to serve.

3. How has faithfully serving others brought you happiness?

4. How does someone remain usable without becoming a doormat? How do you identify the fine line that exists between being abused and being willing to be humble?

5. Have you ever been, as the lesson described Martha, busy doing the Lord's work but lacking in a servant's heart? What could you identify as a warning sign in your life to let you know that is occurring? How could this attitude, when magnified, result in a church's demise?

6. What causes you to get preoccupied with the throne instead of the towel? What kind of mid-course correction can you make when you realize that you are—

- overly competitive?
- jealous?
- resistant to authority?

- petty?
- overly desirous of recognition?

7. In the average course of a day, does the idea that, as the lesson states, "the happiest life is the life of service", actually occur to you? What feelings do you typically have when you are serving? Are they happy ones?

8. Name some examples of modern-day foot-washing. How could more of this be done by your small group or Bible-study fellowship class?

9. Is your church filled with "half-empty people", as the lesson contends some churches are? Are you a half-empty person? Why or why not?

10. What would be required for you to say of yourself, as Gen. William Booth did, "God has had all there was of me"? What kind of personal growth would be needed within yourself before you could honestly make that statement?

Lesson #4

Receive One Another

Romans 14:1-12

In Romans 14 and 15 Paul deals with the problem of division in the church. In this particular fellowship, the believers are divided over diets and days. The weak Christians eat only vegetables; the strong Christians realize that they can eat anything because the Lord Jesus Christ has declared all food clean. The weak Christians will commemorate special holy days, whereas the strong Christians esteem all days as special to the Lord. Sad to say, the weak Christians judge the strong Christians; the strong Christians despise the weak Christians. Romans 15:1 says, *We then who are strong ought to bear with the scruples of the weak, and not to please ourselves* (Rom. 15:1).

In these two chapters Paul gives three admonitions for us to obey if we are to have harmony in the church: *Receive one another* (14:1-2), *edify one another* (14:13-23), and *please one another* (15:1-7).

Christians do not always agree. They do not agree about religious celebrations, religious practices, or styles of worship. If you start arguing about areas of disagreement, you could divide a church a dozen ways. We allow ourselves to be divided over Bible translations and over participating in certain ministries or amusements. Paul lays down a very practical admonition: *Receive one another, and don't argue. Receive one another but not for the purpose of carrying on disputes.* He is writing, of course, about receiving people into the local fellowship. He is discussing Christians who are disagreeable about their disagreements.

The weak Christians, of course, are the ones who are all wrapped up in rules and regulations. The weak Christians in the fellowship probably have been saved out of Judaism; they are still devoted to the law of the Old Testament. The strong Christians realize that Jesus Christ represents freedom from the Old Testament ceremonial law but not from the moral law. The righteousness of the law still is God's standard. According to Romans 8:1-4 the righteousness of the law is being fulfilled in us by the Holy Spirit as we walk in the Spirit. But we are not obligated to obey all the details of the Old Testament ceremonial law given through Moses. The strong Christians enjoy their liberty and despise the legalistic, weak Christians. The weak Christians continue in their immaturity and condemn the strong Christians.

This situation reminds me of a big brother and a little brother. The big brother has privileges the little brother does not have. If the little brother dared to do some of the things that the big brother did, this would hurt him. But the big brother looks down on the little brother and says, "You're just a little kid; you can't do the things I do!"

Sometimes I see that attitude in churches in which strong Christians are careless and even defiant in their relationship to weaker and younger Christians. This leads to disputing, despising, and even denouncing or judging. It is not a happy, healthy situation.

Paul gives four very practical reasons why we are to receive one another and not argue with one another about these minor, non-essential differences. Please keep in mind that I am not talking about major, essential doctrines. I am not talking about the incarnation of Jesus Christ, the resurrection, or the inspiration of Scripture. These are cardinal, fundamental doctrines about which all Christians must agree. I am talking about minor matters about which Christians often disagree.

I. God has received us.

> 1 *Receive one who is weak in the faith, but not to disputes over doubtful things.*
>
> 2 *For one believes he may eat all things, but he who is weak eats only vegetables.*
>
> 3 *Let not him who eats despise him who does not eat, and let not him who does not eat judge him who eats; for God has received him* (Rom. 14:1-3).

If God the Father has received me into His family, what right do you have to reject me? If the Father has received you into the family, what right do I have to reject you?

Remember that in Acts, God speaks to Peter and says, "Peter, I want you to go to the Gentiles . . ." (Acts 10). Peter says, "Not so, Lord! They are unclean." God says, "You don't call anyone *unclean* that I have declared clean." So Peter goes to the Gentiles and preaches the gospel. The group to which he preaches accepts Christ as Savior. A wonderful blessing descends on the household of Cornelius. The church in Jerusalem hears about this new movement and calls Peter on the carpet (Acts 11). Peter's reply is simply, "*The Holy Spirit came upon them just as He did upon us, and they trusted Christ. Therefore, since God has accepted them I have to accept them*" (Acts 11:15-17).

The Jewish Christians then say, "Isn't this marvelous? God has given the gift of repentance to the Gentiles." Paul goes out to minister to the Gentiles. He arrives home to report that God has opened a door of faith to the Gentiles. But some of the legalistic Jewish believers want to close that door! When God has received someone, you have to receive him or her also. You may have disagreements with the person, but you have to receive him or her. The first reason for receiving one another is that God has received us.

Did you know the Bible says that God considers born-again believers trophies of His grace and gifts to His Son? You see the value God the Father places on every one of us. God cares about us; we matter to Him! In Jesus' high-priestly prayer He says the Father loves us like He loves Jesus! (John 17:21-23).

To offer acceptance to someone as an act of kindness is the wrong motivation, because right at the heart of that kindness will be a form of condescension. Such condescension might not be consciously intended, but the person receiving it will quickly perceive it as such. The "down-and-out" person at a homeless shelter may appreciate what is being done for him, but he will know that these Christians, though friendly, will never be his friends. The reason why they won't is because of this condescension, unstated and secretly contemplated. If pointed out, it is often vehemently denied. Nevertheless it exists. How radically this perception would be altered, though, if the extender of this acceptance had the conviction that within that other believer is a glory so good that if he could see it as Jesus sees it, he just like Jesus would have this thought, this motivation, this expectation constantly on His mind.

The reality is that all believers have the new nature of Jesus. Everything the law commands—everything righteousness demands is satisfied by the new nature we receive at spiritual birth. Measure this new nature; this alone is who the believer really is. That is the Christ-life that all believers possess.

The implication the new nature has for establishing the worthiness of a believer and for establishing our receiving of one another is enormous. If we ever get hold of this truth, and even better, if this truth ever gets hold of us, it will cause us to be much more motivated to extend a big-hearted acceptance toward others.

Remember that acceptance is not approval. I may receive you as my brother or sister in Christ and not approve of a certain behavior. Acceptance does not depend on resolving all our differences but on reconciling that we are family in Christ.

How sad that in the church more attention often is given to what divides us rather than what unites us. This is true in almost every relationship setting. A counselor asks a husband and wife at the point of divorce each to make one list describing what they love, admire, and appreciate most about the spouse and on the other a list of things they dislike and frustrate them about the person. Which list typically is the longest? In all my years of asking couples to undertake this activity, more than 90 percent of the lists that are the longest are the ones that enumerate positive affirmations. So why is the focus on the positive list? Because at the heart of all conflict is self-centeredness.

Here's a historical account of how such division can occur in the family of God. During their early years together, John Wesley and George Whitefield were good friends. In fact, Wesley began his ministry of outdoor revivals because of Whitefield's encouragement. In later years, however, the two fell into major disagreement. A theological dispute drove a wedge in their friendship.

When George Whitefield later died, someone approached Wesley and he began the conversation with, "I don't . . .." A pause then occurred. The inquirer thought that the overflow of his long-standing dispute was about to surface again. Then Wesley continued with tears in his eyes, "He'll be so near the throne of God that men like me will never even get a glimpse of him." Grace had taken over, unity had prevailed, and the years of division now must have seemed so senseless and wasted.

I am amazed how some Christians, especially those in leadership and even pastors, can live with a "my-way-or-the-highway attitude." They celebrate "backdoor" revivals. They look at someone and say, "Well, we can do without you; we don't need you in our fellowship." This is a dangerous thing to say and lacks the spirit of love we find in Christ. In our new nature it should not be natural. The person that we do not receive—who has the right to be received—may be just the one we really need. God sustains the person; therefore, we should receive him or her.

II. Jesus Christ is Lord.

> 5 *One person esteems one day above another; another esteems every day alike. Let each be fully convinced in his own mind.*
>
> 6 *He who observes the day, observes it to the Lord; and he who does not observe the day, to the Lord he does not observe it. He who eats, eats to the Lord, for he gives God thanks; and he who does not eat, to the Lord he does not eat, and gives God thanks.*
>
> 7 *For none of us lives to himself, and no one dies to himself.*
>
> 8 *For if we live, we live to the Lord; and if we die, we die to the Lord. Therefore, whether we live or die, we are the Lord's.*
>
> 9 *For to this end Christ died and rose and lived again, that He might be Lord of both the dead and the living* (Rom. 14:5-9).

Eight times the word *Lord* is used. Jesus is Lord; I am not. I am not Lord over any person; no person is Lord over me. Jesus Christ is the Lord. He is the Lord by nature because He is God; He is Lord by right because He died for us and rose again that He might be Lord.

I fear that too many "junior gods" are running around in the average church today. Some weak Christians seemingly cannot do a thing unless they check with somebody else. Having guidance from mature believers is good, but God says that Jesus is Lord. Don't let any person take the place of God in your life.

In John 21:19 the Lord Jesus says to Peter, "*Follow me*." So Peter begins to follow the Lord. Then Peter hears footsteps behind him, so he turns around. That is a dangerous thing to do; he takes his eyes off Jesus and sees John. Peter asks the Lord, "*Lord, and what shall this man do?*" Jesus answers, "*What is that to you? Follow me*."

I do not have the right to tell you what God wants to do in your life. I can pray for you, I can counsel you, I can show you what God's Word says, but I cannot take the place of God in your life. Weak, immature Christians are always looking for crutches, props, and substitutes. Mature Christians realize that Jesus is Lord. Because Jesus is Lord, we cannot criticize one another or argue with one another about trifles. He is Lord!

III. Jesus is the judge.

> 10 *But why do you judge your brother? Or why do you show contempt for your brother? For we shall all stand before the judgment seat of Christ.*
>
> 11 *For it is written: "As I live, says the Lord, every knee shall bow to Me, and every tongue shall confess to God."*

12 *So then each of us shall give account of himself to God* (Rom. 14:10-12).

I will not be sitting on the judgment seat of Christ, nor will you. Jesus will. You will stand there to answer for your own life and not for others' decisions. Jesus alone is the judge. The Lord is not going to ask you to give an account of me, nor will He ask me to give an account of you. I must give an account for myself; so must you. If we spend less time criticizing one another, judging one another, or making decisions for one another and spend more time judging ourselves and evaluating our own lives, we would be in better shape to stand before the Judgment Seat of Christ.

Some questions to consider:

1. What kinds of minor, nonessential differences divide people in congregations today? How does this apply to families? What are some of the minor, nonessential things over which families squabble?

2. In what ways do you accept other people? How does this differ with the biblical basis for receiving other Christians?

3. Think of a time that you have not been "received" well—that you have experienced rejection for one reason or another. On a scale of one to five (1 being almost none, and 5 being a great deal), to what extent has that rejection or possible rejection impacted you? What did you do about it? What did you learn from it?

4. Have you ever been in a church situation in which you found that you were not a good "fit" . . . that the church body of which you were a part (or, your particular small group or area of ministry) was not "receiving" you as the Scripture directs? What

did you do? How does one know whether "moving on"—changing churches or finding another small group of ministry that is a better fit within your current church—is the right thing to do in such a circumstance versus staying put and working within the current situation?

5. How easily do you remember that God loves another person (especially one you find difficult to love) as much as He loves Jesus? How would remembering this concept more readily affect how you treat those that you struggle to like?

6. How would your relationships be altered if you viewed other believers through "lenses" that allow you to see the new nature that each person received with the new birth?

7. How do you differentiate between "acceptance" and "approval"? In what kinds of situations might you accept a new believer as one with you in Christ yet not approve of that person's actions?

8. What kinds of "my-way-or-the-highway" attitudes do you identify in your own life? Can you reflect on any personal experience in which this attitude has harmed relationships?

9. Have you ever done as the lesson mentions—played "junior God"—exerted undue influences on people, especially in the church setting? What was the result? How can you envision that this could bring harm to the body of Christ?

10. The illustration from John 21:19 the lesson mentions about Peter and John has often been considered a classic biblical illustration of codependency. How difficult is it for you to make a decision based on what's correct for you (based on your awareness of God's plan for your life) without looking to the right or left in terms of what other people think?

11. How can you encourage other Christians to make decisions on their own without having to lean on emotional crutches or props? What might some of those emotional props be?

12. Can you think of a time in which you have tried to make a decision for someone else or "reap the whirlwind" of a bad decision instead of letting that person stand on his or her own two feet or suffer logical consequences of his or her actions? What was the result? How can this type of action harm relationships within a home? within a church body?

Lesson #5

Edify One Another

Romans 14:14-21

14 *I know and am convinced by the Lord Jesus that there is nothing unclean of itself; but to him who considers anything to be unclean, to him it is unclean.*

15 *Yet if your brother is grieved because of your food, you are no longer walking in love. Do not destroy with your food the one for whom Christ died.*

16 *Therefore do not let your good be spoken of as evil;*

17 *for the kingdom of God is not eating and drinking, but righteousness and peace and joy in the Holy Spirit.*

18 *For he who serves Christ in these things is acceptable to God and approved by men.*

19 *Therefore let us pursue the things which make for peace and the things by which one may edify another.*

20 *Do not destroy the work of God for the sake of food. All things indeed are pure, but it is evil for the man who eats with offense.*

21 *It is good neither to eat meat nor drink wine nor do anything by which your brother stumbles or is offended or is made weak* (Rom. 14:14-21).

Christians who care edify one another. The word *edify* means "to build up." It is from the Latin word which means "to build". Our English word *edifice* is from the same word. Loving Christians build up one another in the faith.

In our fellowship we are to minister to one another. One way we minister to one another is by edifying one another.

The world has two kinds of people in it—those who build up and those who tear down—those who speak life and those who speak death. Tearing down takes very little effort and very little intelligence, but something is required of you to build up another person. Being a destroyer is much easier than is being a builder, but God wants us to be builders. He does not want us to go through life tearing down other people, churches, or Sunday-school classes. He wants us to edify one another.

Our example

God has given us several spiritual vehicles that we can use for building up one another. The first vehicle for edifying one another is our example. In Romans 14 Paul discusses the problem of disagreement concerning Christians. Last week we considered *receiving one another*; today we consider what *edifying one another* is. This is a recurring theme in Paul's letters to the church. In 1 Thessalonians 5:11 he instructs us to *edify one another*. This implies that none of us is to reach a plateau and camp out there. Yet many Christians—perhaps most Christians—do precisely that. After an initial flurry of excitement and small surge of spiritual growth, a sizeable percentage of believers go no further than where their first steps from conversion took them. Not wanting this to be the pattern in His church, Jesus gives every believer the assignment to help other believers grow.

The object of this edification is to help believers move from the natural person—the carnal person—to the spiritual person. We must go from being babies to becoming young men and women to becoming adults; this usually involves being parents. Which of these three buildings best characterizes your spiritual status? It's not that we don't recognize our status; we just become accustomed to it.

Driving across a city and through a ghetto we are moved to ask, "Why don't people move their families from here?" Obviously economic reasons exist, but sociologists tell us that a major reason people are not interested in moving is because their present situation is the only environment they've ever known. In other words, it's home. For the same reason many people live in spiritual slums.

Just as the ghetto needs people and resources to build up destroyed structures, the church needs "soul-builders." We place a lot of emphasis on "soul-winning", as we should; it's a mandate from God, but we also need to connect with other believers so they may be built up in the body of Christ.

The age-old problem in the church is that we "dip them, then drop them." As I look at the progression of discipleship, I see clearly that many Christians need to be delivered before they can be discipled. Many believers simply don't know how to do life, let alone live the victorious Christian life.

Our calling is to meet believers where they are and build on the foundation of Jesus Christ. The church must balance evangelism and edification. Why? Because the quality of our spiritual lives is an important issue to the Lord. Therefore, we must be intentional on becoming fully committed disciples of Jesus Christ and then intentional in making disciples for Christ. We must not only desire to produce fruit but desire to produce much fruit. In producing "much fruit", God is glorified.

God has called us to be disciple-makers, or "soul-builders."

This requires us to be involved in other people's lives. Carnality in a believer's life is unacceptable.

I. The purpose

> 3 *As I urged you when I went into Macedonia—remain in Ephesus that you may charge some that they teach no other doctrine,*
> 4 *nor give heed to fables and endless genealogies, which cause disputes rather than godly edification which is in faith.*
> 5 *Now the purpose of the commandment is love from a pure heart, from a good conscience, and from sincere faith . . .* (1 Tim. 1:3-5).

The commandment to which Paul refers here is the command to drop the genealogy debates and to commit instead to godly edification. Paul says this edification should target three results—all of them expressions of God's love, which is the one part of the Holy Spirit's fruit that sums up all the other parts. The first outcome or objective Paul mentions is a pure heart. Purity of heart is that sensitivity of soul that hates sin and loves righteousness. Billy Graham once observed that some of the things that would have shocked us 20 years ago are taken in stride today. The incessant bombardment of the world's stimuli has weakened our moral defenses and conditioned us to accept what we would never accept if we were standing in the presence of the Lord of glory.

The second goal of edifying is a good conscience. Have you ever heard the statement, "Let your conscience be your guide"? The only way that statement has any value or truth is if your conscience has been reprogrammed by the Word of God and the

Holy Spirit has full access to activate our consciences. In 1 Corinthians 8:12 Paul warns us of a *weak conscience*; in Hebrews 10:22 he warns of an *evil conscience*, and in 1 Timothy 4:2 of a *seared conscience*.

The pure conscience is one that at the right time sounds the alarm loud, long, and clear. Knowing that we can render our consciences inoperative by neglecting or rejecting what they have to say is a scary thing.

The third goal of edification ministry is a sincere faith. The church is full of double-minded people. Double-mindedness vacillates between reason and revelation, between feeling and faith. James says, *Let not that man think* (the one who is double -minded) *that he will receive anything from the Lord* (Jas. 1:7). Double-mindedness leads to hypocrisy. As is often stated from our pulpits, "We believe in God, we just don't believe God." Paul urges us to walk by faith and not by sight, to be sense/sight-oriented instead of spirit/faith-oriented, and to be problem-conscious instead of promise-conscious; which is to set ourselves up to misread the situation entirely.

II. The provision

A. Our example

If I am going to be a disciplemaker, I first of all must be a disciple myself. In the post-modern age and the rise of the emerging church we hear less and less about disciples of Christ and more and more about Christ-followers. In my opinion this is more than semantics. The New Testament is filled with word pictures of the crowds who followed Jesus but who never committed their lives to Jesus. That's why Jesus, in His Sermon on the Mount, gave such a clear picture of the true disciple of Christ. I encourage you to read my book, *Radical Disciples . . . Are You Really a Christian?*

B. Our speech

The second means we have for building up others is our speech. Ephesians 4:29 says, *Let no corrupt word proceed out of your mouth, but what is good for necessary edification, that it may impart grace to the hearers.* You cannot see spoken words. We can attach electronic devices to a microphone; then we can see the impact of the words electrically, but we cannot see the actual spoken words. Words have power. Words are able to build up or to tear down. Have you ever had the experience of someone visiting you on a dark, dismal day and merely speaking a word of encouragement? On the other hand, have you ever had the experience of someone criticizing you when you were otherwise feeling fine? Perhaps you received a letter that was critical; the sun suddenly disappeared. Words have power!

Ephesians 4:15 says *but, speaking the truth in love, may grow up in all things into Him who is the head—Christ.* We need both truth and love. As we speak the truth in love, we are able to build people up. Someone has said that love without truth is hypocrisy and truth without love is brutality. We do not want either of these. We want to speak the truth in love. Our words should minister grace to those that hear them. Our speech should always be, as Colossians 4:6 says, *with grace, seasoned with salt* . . .. We are always to have a generousness about our speech that springs from a heart filled with love. We edify one another by our example and by our speech.

C. Our spiritual gifts

> 12 *Even so you, since you are zealous for spiritual gifts, let it be for the edification of the church that you seek to excel . . .*
>
> 26 *How is it then, brethren? Whenever you come together, each of you has a psalm, has a teaching, has a*

tongue, has a revelation, has an interpretation. Let all things be done for edification (1 Cor. 14:12; 26).

As you know, the Corinthian church to which this passage refers is consumed with spiritual gifts. Members compete with each other. The Corinthians form a very gifted church; in fact, Paul states that they did not *lack any gift* (1 Cor. 1:4-17). But they are using those gifts as toys to play with and as weapons to fight with, not as tools with which to build. They are comparing and competing with one another. They are "showing off with their spiritual gifts." God gives us spiritual gifts—not to show off and not to build up our own egos but to build up one another.

In fact, the services held by the Corinthian assembly are not "building-up oriented" at all. They are "tearing-down oriented." In 1 Corinthians 11:17 Paul says, *When you meet together it is not for the better but for the worse*. Unfortunately when some of God's people get together, rivalry, bickering, and competition instead of unity occur. People go home not having been built up but having been torn down. *Let all things be done for edification* (1 Cor. 14:26).

This means that when the church gathers together, the hymns and songs should be edifying and the teaching and preaching should be edifying. Even the visiting and eating together should be edifying.

Our spiritual gifts are given to us not for our own benefit but for the benefit of the body. Again, I encourage you to also read my book, *The Steps to a Transformed Life*. We need to understand and know what our spiritual gifts are.

God wants to use each of us as building blocks in the Body of Christ, the church. The average church member is ignorant about his or her own spiritual giftedness. In discovering my gift and that of others, I am able to help my brothers and sisters grow in Christ.

D. Our love

God gives us a fourth vehicle for building up one another. In 1 Corinthians 8:1 Paul says, *Knowledge puffeth up, but charity edifieth*. Love edifies.

All of us know people who are smart, but all they do is tear things down. They know the Word of God, but it has become a weapon they use as they go from church to church. Paul says in effect, "You have knowledge; that is fine. But knowledge will puff up and inflate your ego. Love will build up." He is not saying that we have to make a choice between love and knowledge, because God wants us to speak the truth in love. He is saying, sing your song in love. Whatever you are doing for God, do it in love. Love always builds up.

This means I must have the love of God in my heart. This all relates to what Jesus says to His disciples in John 13:34, "*A new commandment I give you, that you love one another.*" Building people up in hatred, in criticism, or in strife is impossible

E. Our prayer

Colossians 4:12 says, *Epaphras, who is one of you, a bondservant of Christ, greets you, always laboring fervently for you in prayers, that you may stand perfect and complete in all the will of God* (Col. 4:12).

As we pray for people, then God is able to work and to build them up. We build up each other through prayer. I hope you have written down a list of people for whom you are praying. As I specifically pray for others, I can see God moving in my world.

F. God's Word

In Acts 20:32 Paul says, *And now, brethren, I commend you to God, and to the word of grace, which is able to build you up*. The Word of God is the greatest vehicle for building up one another. When you discuss people's problems with them, use God's Word. When folks call to complain about something, use the Word of God. Drop the Word of God into your conversation. Share the Word of God. Don't go around beating people over the head with the Bible; don't go around quoting Scripture all the time, but do use the Word of God discreetly, because it builds people up.

To experience what God calls "great giving" so that one day we will be about to live in a mansion of maturity, we need more "soul-builders" in the church. Within the church needs to be a camaraderie of construction, not of physical buildings, but what is much more valuable—an ongoing construction of personal lives! We need to see lives being built up in such an impressive way that everyone feels special to be a part of something so great! We need lives that draw the attention of the world by displaying qualities only God can produce! We need lives that bring the Father deserved glory and ready the church for her marriage to His Son!

You don't want to go from year to year with little evidence of spiritual growth—that uneasy feeling inside you which prefers to change the subject rather than to focus on the extent of your spiritual growth. This should be so—you can grow! Your life can count! Instead of languishing in defeat or drifting without purpose, you can have a steady and even stunning building up of your life, if this is what you really want. Don't you want Jesus to view you with admiration—to take pride in how you have turned out—to use you as an example of what the abundant life looks like?

Some questions to consider:

1. Which description most accurately describes your present level of spiritual growth?

- A mansion.
- A tract home.
- A fixer-upper.
- A ghetto.

2. Of the edification goals—pure heart, good conscience, and sincere faith—which one most needs to develop in your life?

3. What is your spiritual gift? How can you use it to build up other believers?

4. Describe a time in which you have used the Word of God in your conversation to edify others. What was the result?

5. How can you determine whether you are using your knowledge of Scripture to build up or tear down others? How do you know whether you are using Scripture to be critical versus to speak the truth in love?

6. What would be necessary for you to watch your words more carefully so that they only edify? If you don't already do this, what would be involved in your developing the discipline of editing your words before you speak them?

7. Does the Holy Spirit have full access to activate your conscience? Do you have some areas in your life in which you have compartmentalized—shut off the ability of the Holy Spirit's ability to convict you of wrong?

8. What can you personally do to help other believers grow? What specific ministries can you participate in in your church to help "deliver" believers from the world so they can thoroughly enjoy all that the Christ-life has to offer?

9. Do you see any evidence in your life of tearing down another instead of building another up—being a destroyer rather

than a builder? What habits do you have that you need to jettison to follow more fully the biblical command to *edify one another*—to be a Christian who cares?

10. What can you do to become a "soul-builder"—one who genuinely becomes involved in others' lives for the purpose of improving the quality of the spiritual lives of those around you?

Lesson #6

Do Not Judge One Another

Romans 14:3, 13

> *Therefore let us not judge one another anymore* (Rom. 14:13).

Christians who care do not judge one another. Romans 14:3 says, *Let not him who eats despise him who does not eat, and let not him who does not eat judge him who eats; for God has received him* (Rom. 14:3). The truth is that a great deal of judging goes on in this world and even in the church. I sometimes sense that among Christians, judging is the most popular "indoor" sport. The Bible sets down some essential guidelines about this Christian admonishment. God not only is interested in what we do to and for other believers, He is concerned about what we are not to do.

I am sure judging has always been a reality among human relationships; early on in His public ministry Jesus addresses it. During the centuries that divide the Testaments, the Pharisees emerge on the religious scene as a strong and respected voice. Under their leadership hundreds of laws are added to complement the Mosaic laws. In them we see the idea that "if I can't keep God's moral laws, I will make some I can keep." At the heart of religion you will find rules and regulations. The essence of all false religion is, "I will somehow please God by my works." False religion says "human achievement"; Christianity says "divine accomplishment." We are not saved by these works but by the sacrifice of Jesus on the cross and His literal resurrection.

Hopefully we get that! This lesson's focus is not on the eternal truths of election that produces salvation. Naturally, this positional view gives us our eternal hope. The focus is on what brings us into the intimacy of our relationship with Christ or what brings a wedge in between that intimacy. I am not addressing judicial forgiveness that happens at our spiritual birth but parental forgiveness that brings us into intimate fellowship with God.

Jesus says when we judge others wrongly, a judgment enters our lives that diminishes our fellowship with God. Therefore, we must define what constitutes *judging*. Judging has nothing to do with calling sin *sin*. If I see you drink liquor and you are unable to speak clearly or to walk a straight line, I am not judging if I say, "You are drunk." That simply is an honest evaluation of your condition. Jesus points out that these Pharisees who hold everyone's feet to the fire to implicitly follow the rules and humanity's religious traditions are themselves *hypocrites*, a *brood of vipers*, and a *white-coated sepulcher*. Jesus always calls sin *sin*! I can judge rightly when I discriminate between truth and error, right and wrong. This is not what the Bible forbids.

The judging that judges by God

The classic text for gaining understanding is found in Matthew 7:1-5,

> 1 "*Judge not, that you be not judged.*
> *2 For with what judgment you judge, you will be judged; and with the measure you use, it will be meas-*

ured back to you.

3 And why do you look at the speck in your brother's eye, but do not consider the plank in your own eye?

4 Or how can you say to your brother, 'Let me remove the speck from your eye'; and look, a plank is in your own eye?

5 Hypocrite! First remove the plank from your own eye, and then you will see clearly to remove the speck from your brother's eye."

This is not the judgment of God about believers at the judgment seat of Christ, which in reality is a place of rewarding believers, nor the judgment of sinners at the final pronouncement of hell at the Great White Throne Judgment. Jesus is referring to the judgment of person upon person on this earth. Jesus is saying that if we prefer condemnation to commendation, then that's exactly what we'll get. We'll be measured by our own yardstick and be compelled to buy on the same scale with which we sell. The focus is not on our judging the reality of sin, because we as believers are called on to deal with sin in our lives and in other believers' lives by teaching, exhorting, admonishing, and rebuking.

In Matthew 18, Jesus calls on believers to take steps to help sinning believers to repent and be restored into fellowship with Jesus and His church. One does not judge when he or she goes to other believers committing scriptural sin and confronting them with the Scripture that defines their sin. In Galatians 6 Paul tells us that the spiritual brother has an obligation to go to sinning believers seeking to realize their sin so that they will repent and be restored into fellowship.

The spiritual Christian's approach to a believer involved in sin is as follows:

1. Only confront scriptural sin (not personal conviction) of which you have personal knowledge.

2. Go to the person individually and privately. This is not with the idea to make the person's sin something of a public spectacle. If the individual refuses to repent, the process should then continue with two or three other believers who have personal knowledge of the sin. This is not responding to "hearsay".

3. After exhausting every effort to restore, at some point the sinning brother's lack of repentance must be brought before the church. Fellowship must be removed until such time that repentance takes place. The church leadership and not the entire church body is to deal with this issue. The church would simply be made aware that church discipline has been administered.

Church discipline is done out of love; punishment is done out of revenge. The idea is not to remove the sinning person but to restore him or her into fellowship with the Lord and His church. Speaking the truth in love is an act of love. Only holiness can lead to happiness. A sinning believer will face the discipline of God that brings him or her discouragement, dislocation, and possibly premature death. The Bible says for believers there is a *sin unto death*. Church discipline is also done out of a love for the church. Church discipline reminds all believers, "Choose to sin, choose to suffer." The law of sowing and reaping is a divine law that will break or bless a believer, depending on what the believer is sowing.

Why is judging another believer wrong?

First of all, because I have an equal perspective. The problem is, "I hate your sin; my sin is not that bad." We have a way of justifying our shortcomings and amplifying everyone else's. We all have a set of biases that distorts our perspective. Jesus says we see the speck in another person's eye but can't see the log in our own. Frankly, pointing out your sin is much easier than is dealing with my own. Secondly, while we may easily see the obvious, what we can't see is another person's motive. Only God can judge our motives. For me to adhere to religious practices but have God judge my wrong motives is possible. I can't know your motive nor you mine.

Working out at the gym I noticed an older man of 50 or 60 working out with a younger woman. He had his hands all over her. He was constantly touching her hand, which from my perspective was totally inappropriate. I was judging the entire situation until I got a different perspective. The reality was that he was a professional trainer; she was blind. With great effort he was helping her accomplish what she could never have done on her own. "*Judge not!*" We don't have God's perspective; we can't see the motive. Unless you are willing to deal with your own sin, you are disqualified to deal with anyone else's.

The Christian life requires discernment. Christian love is not blind. Paul prayed for the Philippians, *And this I pray, that your love may abound yet more and more in knowledge and in all judgment* (discernment); *that you may approve things that are excellent; that you be sincere and without offense till the day of Christ* (Phil. 1:9 10). His prayer is that we might have loving, clear, and careful discernment. We are to exercise love with honest discernment. In the Sermon on the Mount Jesus warns us, "*Don't cast your pearls before swine. Don't give that which is holy to the dogs*" (Matt. 7:6). I have to discern who are the pig, dog, and sheep. We do not distribute the measures of grace of God indiscriminately. We must exercise discernment. However, discernment, if we are not careful, can turn into a judgmental attitude. In trying to be true to God, we may get so critical, so judgmental, so condemning that nothing is right except what we do. Nothing is good except what we like.

We must start with ourselves. In the Bible we are not told that helping a brother by pointing out his weakness is wrong. What we are told is that we are to start by examining ourselves.

> 37 *"Judge not, and you shall not be judged. Condemn not, and you shall not be condemned. Forgive, and you will be forgiven.*
>
> 38 *Give, and it will be given to you: good measure, pressed down, shaken together, and running over will be put into your bosom. For with the same measure that you use, it will be measured back to you"* (Luke 6:37-38).

What we plant, we get back; we reap much more than we plant. That's the law of the harvest. God holds me to the standard to which I hold others. I have not always followed this principle and have suffered for it. Before I criticize you, I need to see if something even worse exists in my own life. When I am willing to start with myself, I see my brother's life more clearly; I have more compassion. I don't want a doctor doing surgery on my eye with a crowbar and a pipe wrench. I want tenderness, delicacy, and compassion, because my eye is super-sensitive and highly important to my living. So we don't rush up to people to condemn or judge. We first examine our own lives to see whether we find something with which we need to deal. Jesus wants us to help other believers, but remember: He alone is God.

> 9 *For to this end Christ died and rose and lived again, that He might be Lord of both the dead and the living.*
>
> 10 *But why do you judge your brother? Or why do you show contempt for your brother? For we shall all stand before the judgment seat of Christ* (Rom. 14:9-10).

Paul is talking about weak Christians judging strong Christians. I am not the Holy Spirit who alone can convict of sin, righteousness, and judgment. I am not Jesus Who alone has the right and perspective to judge what's in another person's heart.

> 14 *I know and am convinced by the Lord Jesus that there is nothing unclean of itself; but to him who considers anything to be unclean, to him it is unclean.*
>
> 15 *Yet if your brother is grieved because of your food, you are no longer walking in love. Do not destroy with your food the one for whom Christ died* (Rom. 14:14-15).

Letting rules, regulations, and religious traditions become factors in determining whether someone is sinning is easy. Operating out of legalism is easier than is living in grace. I have very strong opinions about certain things and sensitive convictions about other things. While these things are very important to me and by God's grace I can live by the dictates of my own heart, it does not mean everyone adheres to them. Different is not necessarily wrong; it's just different. I must not bring disunity into the body or hinder the work of the Lord for the sake of my own prejudices and opinions.

1 *We then who are strong ought to bear with the scruples of the weak, and not to please ourselves.*
2 *Let each of us please his neighbor for his good, leading to edification* (Rom. 15:1-2).

Always show patience and love. We first celebrate what we have in the unity of Christ. As much as possible, strong Christians who are walking in the freedom of God ought to please the weak Christians so they can lovingly help them grow. Parents do this all the time. We adjust our plans for the schooling of our children; we adjust our living to the weakness of our children. Strong Christians in the fellowship have to consider the weak Christians and not selfishly please themselves.

So we need discernment. We must start with ourselves when judging is concerned. We must have priorities; we don't destroy God's work for something unimportant. In setting our priorities for Christian action we can ask ourselves the question, "Will this matter one second inside eternity?" We must show love and patience. As much as possible, try to please the weaker Christians for their good.

Exercising judgment is not wrong; being judgmental is. Having discernment is not wrong; we must have it. But we are wrong if we think we are are the only ones who are right. We must remember that Jesus is Lord. The lordship of Christ solves so many problems. Forsake a judgmental attitude.

Some questions to consider:

1. What is the difference in evaluating reality and being judgmental?

2. What is the one thing about another believer that only God can judge?

3. What is the difference between judging and church discipline?

4. What instruction did Jesus give in Matthew 18 about dealing with a sinning believer?

5. How do you feel when you realize that your fellowship with God is diminished when you judge others?

6. Have you ever approached a believer about his or her being involved in a scriptural sin? What was the result? How did you communicate love to the person while at the same time pointing out error?

7. How do you respond to the statement, "Only holiness can lead to happiness"? Have you found this to be true in your life? Can you give an example of how you have seen this enacted?

8. Have you ever judged a person only to learn that he or she had a motive that explained everything adequately? What happened?

9. How can you take steps toward personally accepting the concept that "different is not wrong; it's just different"? Can you think of times in your life in which being critical of people's "differentness" has caused heartache for you?

10. What are some ways in which your judgmental attitude has been injurious in a church situation?

11. What would be necessary for you to adopt an attitude of "cleaning up your own back yard" first before you criticize others?

Lesson #7

Bear One Another's Burdens

Galatians 6:1-5

Have you ever heard the saying, "I love the world; it's the people I can't stand"? The human spirit has an amazing ability to compartmentalize. While we're thinking lofty and noble thoughts, we're fond of saying how much we love others and how willing we are to do anything that might help! Once we parachute into reality and are compelled to deal with certain people we know, suddenly our undying love dies. All our good intentions go right out the window. This often is the way things are when fellowship is involved. Fellowship sounds good in the abstract, but once the fog of generalities begins to lift, and once the specifics of what fellowship really requires enters into view, precisely then is when our lofty ideas get put to the test.

> "To dwell above with those we love
> Oh, that will be glory.
> But to live below with those we know
> Well, that's a different story."

God knows that we have an easier time perceiving than achieving Christian fellowship. This is why He gives specific, how-to instruction about our relationships with other Christians. See Ephesians 4:1-3 that follows.

1 *I, therefore, the prisoner of the Lord, beseech you to walk worthy of the calling with which you were called,*

2 *with all lowliness and gentleness, with longsuffering, bearing with one another in love,*

3 *endeavoring to keep the unity of the Spirit in the bond of peace* (Eph. 4:1-3).

Paul describes the proper attitudes for believers to equip them to bear up one another in love. These are prerequisites for burden-bearing. Notice this starts with me, not the person who has the burden. Humility is the ability to be honest about our strengths and our weaknesses. We are all made up of strengths and weaknesses. Understanding that I have weaknesses balances my ego and keeps me from believing that I have it all together. I often say it like this, "Nobody is as cool as they look!" When I get a grip on who I am, I can reach out with gentleness. We are more understanding of others after we are honest about our own weaknesses. But we also have much to offer because we all have strengths. We are willing to go the extra mile as we patiently walk the walk of life with our brothers and sisters in the Lord.

What is a *burden*?

A contradiction seems to exist between Galatians 6:2 and 6:5, but it really doesn't. In Galatians 6:2 the word for *burdens* refers to a heavy load, a trial—something very difficult to bear. In verse 5 the word refers to a little load one might carry on his or her back. It is a word used for a soldier's backpack.

I have certain burdens that only I can bear. I can't pass my responsibilities to others, because I have to fulfill that work myself. I have to be a husband and a father in my home; I must be the right husband and father. I have to do the work that God has called me to do. Every soldier has to shoulder his own pack. Those people who try to give their responsibility to someone else are missing a blessing and disobeying God. So verse 5 is talking about the responsibility of ministry, but verse 2 is talking about the burdens of life that are so heavy to carry—the trials we endure as believers. The admonition is to *bear one another's burdens, and so fulfill the law of Christ*.

For example, the Bible says if a man will not work, he should not eat. I know that in this day of entitlement, that statement is politically incorrect, but it is true. If a person is too lazy to get out of bed and go to work, to turn off the television and go to a job, he is not entitled to eat. He can do without. The Bible says, "won't work," not "can't work." Many simply can't work for many different reasons, or they are working and they have medical bills, etc. Then the Christian community should help them out in their lives. The help they receive is not their entitlement but their blessing. Like the Good Samaritan, we need to reach out and give a helping hand. We can help people carry many burdens. That is one of the beautiful things about the fellowship of the church. As a fellowship together we can help each other. We are better together! We can help one another materially, physically, financially, and emotionally. We Christians can help to bear burdens in many ways. The particular way Paul is emphasizing here is helping those who have stumbled and fallen. We can help bear up one another spiritually.

Interestingly enough the spiritual burden is the one we shy away from most. No matter how we help bear a burden, the focus is on the heart. Almost always the burdens with which we we called to help represent the result of a person's sinful life, selfish choices, and deceived decisions. No matter what the visible need, we have not successfully helped bear the burden of another if we don't help the person deal with his or her sin. Even if the burden is a direct result of Satanic attack, it is spiritual in nature. To pay a bill for a brother unrepentive of a lifestyle of sinful living is only helping him continue to sin. Is that what the Bible teaches? No! Sin brings its own set of consequences. I am not to get in the way of God's chastening. Even Paul's thorn in the flesh is used of God to check Paul's sin of pride. He gets far more from the thorn in the flesh than he does from the vision of heaven. Dealing with personal sin is a personal issue. No one but me can pray 1 John 1:9 for me. The burden others can and must help me bear is the burden of ministry. Every believer is a minister. I cannot fight the good fight by myself. We are better together; together we can make a difference in our world. The burdens we share include: material (food, money, clothing), physical (sickness, injury), emotional (depression and anxiety), and spiritual (besetting sins) needs.

Do you recall our Lord's words when Lazarus emerges from the tomb? He commands, "*Loose him and let him go!*" Lazarus is a prophet of God's miraculous, supernatural power, as we are! Even so, Lazarus still needs others to help him get free. Aren't we also in need of this help?

How awesome is this burden-bearing ministry! God has given us the privilege of partnering with Him in His resurrected miracle. We are called to help people be set free from their grave clothes.

How to bear another's burdens

> 1 *Brethren, if a man is overtaken in any trespass, you who are spiritual restore such a one in a spirit of gentleness, considering yourself lest you also be tempted.*

2 *Bear one another's burdens, and so fulfill the law of Christ.*

3 *For if anyone thinks himself to be something, when he is nothing, he deceives himself.*

4 *But let each one examine his own work, and then he will have rejoicing in himself alone, and not in another.*

5 *For each one shall bear his own load* (Gal. 6:1-5).

A. What we are to do

We don't rejoice in others' burdens. The word *restore* (v. 1) is not a word about which we are glad. We don't rejoice if someone has sinned, yet some Christians do just that because others' failings make them feel better about themselves. When one member of the body hurts, the entire body hurts.

The Bible does not say we are to "reveal" or expose the sin of fellow believers. Gossip is a concern in the church today. When Noah gets drunk, he lies in his tent naked. Ham laughs at him and makes fun of him (Gen. 9:20-23). Noah's other sons go backward into the tent and cover their father. Love covers a multitude of sins; it doesn't go around revealing them.

Love does not cleanse sin; grace does that. Love does not condone sin, but love does cover sin. We have no reason to hang dirty wash out in public. The Bible does not say, "rejoice" or "reveal". It does not say "reject." It does not say, "if someone falls into sin, reject him, or judge him, or condemn him." The Pharisees do this; they are wrong. The Bible says "restore."

The doctors know this word (*restore*) because it is a medical term used to refer to setting a broken bone. The church is Christ's body. If a member of the church is out of the will of God and out of fellowship with God and falls into sin, this is like having a broken bone. That bone has to be set. The only way to set a broken bone is with tenderness. If it isn't set properly, it is going to create many other problems. I once set my own collarbone; during the last few years I have suffered the result of a job poorly done.

The fisherman knew this word because it meant "to mend the nets." It is translated that way in Matthew 4:21—*mending their nets*. If nets are not mended, you can't use them effectively. If Christians are not mended or restored, God can't use them to catch fish or to serve others.

The soldiers also knew this word. It meant "to equip an army." Unless we help restore those who have sinned, they will never be able to win the battles of life. We aren't just restoring a brother or sister, we are helping equip a soldier to go out and fight the battle.

The sailors knew this word. It meant "to outfit a ship for voyage." Each of us has to face the storms of life. Each of us has to carry cargo for the glory of God. But if the Christian is not restored, he or she cannot do it.

So this word refers to setting a bone, to mending nets, to equipping an army, and to outfitting a ship. That is what we are doing when we help another Christian. We bear one another's burdens when we help to restore a believer who has fallen.

B. Why we are to do it

To fulfill the law of Christ! Do you know what the law of Christ is? John 13:34 says, *A new commandment I give to you, that you love one another; as I have loved you, that you also love one another.* The law of Christ is to love one another. The Golden Rule is to do unto others as you would have them do unto you.

Legalists don't know much about restoring people. A legalist has nothing with which to restore anyone. In the Bible legalists are quick to judge and to condemn, but they have no love in their hearts. If someone does not meet their standards, they have nothing to do with that person.

In Galatians 6:10 Paul addresses his readers. Restoring another Christian is a family matter. We love the members of the family. We are to care for the household of faith. The verse says, *As we have opportunity, let us do good unto all men, especially unto these who are of the household of faith.*

Operating by love and not law is marvelous! The law of love takes care of all other laws. Love is the fulfillment of the law. If we love a person, we can help a brother, we can carry his or her burden, we can help him or her be restored. The way you treat one who has sinned is evidence of your own spiritual condition.

C. How we are to do it

With meekness! Meekness is not weakness. It is power under God's control. A meek person is filled with the Holy Spirit because part of the Fruit of the Spirit is meekness (Gal. 5:22-23). Our blessed Lord says in the beatitudes, "*Blessed are the meek, for they shall inherit the earth*" (Matt. 5:5).

Our illustration of a doctor setting a bone is not a picture of crowbars and pipe wrenches. It is with care and gentleness. We are to have the spirit of meekness because it is power under God's control.

But the main point is this, " . . . *considering yourself, lest you also be tempted*" (v. 1). What we think of ourselves determines how we treat other people. But for God's grace I would be broken and in need of some burden-bearers.

I know we are to cast all our cares on the Lord. When I do, God often uses other people to help meet my deepest needs. When you are bearing burdens, you really are sharing blessings. A Christian is not a burden to another Christian.

Some questions to consider:

1. Contrast what you once considered "bearing burdens" with what you now think this concept consists of.

2 Have you ever helped bear another's burden? If so, describe the experience.

3. Have you ever needed to have someone come along side of you and help you bear your burden? If so, describe.

4. What is the warning found in Galatians 6:1 to mature believers that help a falling brother or sister up?

5. What is the *law of Christ*?

6. Why does being honest about your own weaknesses help you be more understanding of others?

7. What are some practical ways you as a church member can bear others' burdens physically? financially? emotionally?

8. Why is the spiritual burden the one you shy away from most? In your life what would be necessary to make this not the case?

9. How do you sometimes get in the way of God's chastening?

10. Have you ever helped restore a believer who has fallen? What resulted?

Lesson #8

Forgive One Another

Ephesians 4:30-32

An unforgiving spirit creates all kinds of problems. In my pastoral ministry, I have counseled some who have had physical difficulties—not because of sickness, not because of injury, but because of attitudes in their hearts. Many psychiatrists have observed that a person who has emotional problems often has an unforgiving spirit. This is why the Holy Spirit directed Paul to write Ephesians 4:30-32,

> 30 *And do not grieve the Holy Spirit of God, by whom you were sealed for the day of redemption.*
> 31 *Let all bitterness, wrath, anger, clamor, and evil speaking be put away from you, with all malice.*
> 32 *And be kind to one another, tenderhearted, forgiving one another, even as God in Christ forgave you.*

Today we answer some questions about family forgiveness. Remember, Paul was not talking about God's forgiving us so we might obtain salvation; he was talking about family members forgiving one another—those in the church who need to forgive each other. Saying the words, "I forgive you", may be easy enough, but the reality is not what you say with your mouth but what you choose in your heart.

Evidences of an unforgiving saint

A. Corrupt communication

I think the greatest evidence is the way we talk about people. In our text Paul has a great deal to say about speech. For example in Ephesians 4:29 he says, *Let no corrupt communication proceed out of your mouth, but that which is good to the use of edifying (building up), that it may minister grace to the hearers.*

When we have unforgiving spirits, we say things about people that we shouldn't say. Paul talks of *evil speaking*. If I am the kind of person who immediately jumps at the chance to say something evil about a person, that means I am holding a grudge against him or her. One of the first evidences of an unforgiving heart is what you say about people. If I cannot say something good, this may mean that I have something bad in my heart.

B. Inner feelings

Another evidence is bad feelings on the inside. If I don't personally feel forgiven, I am unlikely to be forgiving. Sometimes we are able to control our tongues, bite our lips, and not verbally express what we actually feel about others. My, how people would be shocked if they could see what we feel sometimes in our hearts! Paul speaks of bitterness that infects our hearts. The root of bitterness intertwines its way into every part of your personality. The root of bitterness is to the heart what infection is to the physical body. Some Christians hold things inside; the bitterness just grows like a poison in the system. Bitterness is like drinking poison and waiting for someone else to die, when we are the ones dying from the inside out. No wonder Job says, in effect, "You are only hurting yourself when you are bitter."

As you know, when you have an infection, everything is

very sensitive and everything hurts. Bitterness is an evidence of an unforgiving spirit. Wrath, anger, clamor—these are the outward evidences of that inward feeling. When a fever is in the body, hiding it is awfully difficult. When bitterness is in the heart, you can't hide it. When that person we are bitter toward is mentioned, we become angry, or we decide to say something that we should not say.

So corrupt communication, evil-speaking, bitterness, wrath, anger, and malice all are evidences of an unforgiving spirit. We easily lie in bed at night and think up all sorts of evil things about those who have wronged us! That is another evidence of an unforgiving heart.

When we have this kind of attitude, are we hurting the other person? Of course not! If someone has sinned against me or if someone has done something I didn't like and if I harbor resentment down inside, am I hurting that person? No, I am only hurting myself. Having an unforgiving spirit is something akin to committing spiritual suicide; you are bringing death to your own soul!

Why forgiving is necessary

A. First of all, **we are commanded to do so**. The example is the fact that we have been forgiven. No one will ever need your forgiveness as much as you needed God's. He forgives us totally and completely. We are to obey His command and follow His example.

B. The second reason we are to forgive is **because the failure to do so will block your own relationship to God.** We cannot truly worship God and be in intimate fellowship with God while hating our brother at the same time. This is why Jesus says that if our brother has ought against us, we should leave the place of worship at once and go to our brother to make things right. A forgiving heart can't worship in spirit and in truth and can't pray with fervency. Consider David. In the Bible He says he cannot pray because his sin is ever before him. In the Lord's model prayer Jesus instructs us to pray, " . . . *forgive us our debts as we forgive our debtors*." This not only represents the idea that God allows us to reap what we sow, it also points out that our unwillingness to forgive will reduce our capacity to receive forgiveness. When I refuse to forgive, this takes away my confidence that God in grace has chosen to forgive me. If I can't believe, I can't receive. In this way refusal to forgive can remove us decisively and drastically from the cherished blessings of God.

C. When I refuse to forgive, **this gives Satan a foothold in my life.** An unforgiving spirit not only is Satan's widest door into our hearts, it is his strongest invitation and warmest welcome. Paul warns us not to give Satan a place in our hearts (Eph. 4:27). Whenever we refuse to forgive, we are putting the welcome mat out to Satan. That welcome mat says, "Come on in, devil, and have a rompin', stompin' good time." He will always take us up on that invitation. He will turn a toehold into a stronghold.

D. The failure to forgive **brings great spiritual harm as well as physical and emotional harm to us.** What we eat is not always what makes us physically ill, but what is eating us does. Allowing unforgiveness to eat at you allows people rather than the Holy Spirit to control you. What we refuse to let go of refuses to let go of us also. The wall that shuts out that offending person is the same wall which locks him or her in.

Outwitted

He drew a circle that shut me out—
Heretic, a rebel, a thing to flout.
But Love and I had the wit to win:
We drew a circle that took him in!
(Edwin Markham)

E. Another reason to forgive is that **failure to do so ruins relationships**. Of the 62 biblical references about forgiveness, 22 refer to believers. We are members together in God's family—brothers and sisters in the Lord. We are traveling on the road to glory; why make the trip miserable? How much of God's kingdom work has been marred by disunity that unforgiveness brings? Along the shorelines of God's kingdom work is one sidelined saint after another. Each of them is ruined and wrecked by this refusal to forgive. In 1 John 2:11 the Bible says . . . *he who hates his brother is in darkness and walks in darkness and does not know where he is going* . . .. So, how is that person going to help anyone? He isn't; he can't. C.S. Lewis once said that people consider forgiveness to be such a lovely idea until they have something to forgive! Let's be honest; forgiveness seldom is easy. Even so, we are commanded to forgive. God would never command us to do something that He has not modeled Himself and given us a provision to do so. The prophet says, *The Lord delights in mercy* (Mic. 7:18). Why? Because He knows what tremendous, life-changing benefits forgiveness and mercy bring. Peter asks Jesus, "How many times do we forgive, seven times?" The law requires three, so he must have felt generous. The Lord answers, "Seven times 70." Jesus is not suggesting we walk around with a forgiveness calculator that keeps a record; he simply is suggesting "always." Forgiveness is to be a natural reflex and the instinctive reaction of our heart. Have you ever heard this statement, "I will forgive, but I can never forget"? While forgetting some things is humanly impossible, doing so is not impossible with God. Nothing is! In Jeremiah 31:34 God promises those who approach Him seeking forgiveness, "*I will remember their sin no more.*" God, Who is omniscient, chooses to forget! Forgiven sin according to the Bible is buried in the deepest ocean and cast as far as the east is from the west! We can forgive and God's grace will bless us with fading memories as we choose to see people as God does—with that sin forgiven and with a new nature inside.

Someone once told me that a clear conscience happens because of a poor memory. Have you been able to forget sins and pains of your past? If mothers remember exactly the pain of childbirth, most families would have only one child. The joy of the new life quickly erases the pain of the delivery. In much the same way God's grace works in the heart of the spirit-filled believer. Just as we have an amazing proficiency to forget the pains of life and our own wrongdoings, we can forget offenses toward us. Forgiveness does not mean approval or even trust. The biblical principle of "as they're faithful in little, we will promote them to much" applies. This is not a "prove-yourself mentality" but an unrestricted release of belief that offers a graduated opportunity for that belief in that person to be renewed. It gives personal transformation in the life of that person—the offended party. It reminds the offended party that with God all things are possible.

Essentials for a forgiving heart

The person who will not forgive others destroys the bridge on which he or she may have to walk himself some day. If we do not forgive others, we set up a barrier between us and other people as well as between us and God. In fact, in Matthew 6:15

our Lord Jesus says that forgiving our brother is one condition for answered prayer: *But if you do not forgive men their trespasses, neither will your Father forgive your trespasses.*

A. One essential for a forgiving spirit is **kindness** (Eph. 4:32). Have you ever really stopped to think how kind God is to you? Titus 3 describes what we once were like before we were saved,

> 3 *For we ourselves were also once foolish, disobedient, deceived, serving various lusts and pleasures, living in malice and envy, hateful and hating one another.*
> 4 *But when the kindness and the love of God our Saviour toward man appeared,*
> 5 *not by works of righteousness which we have done, but according to His mercy He saved us, through the washing of regeneration and renewing of the Holy Spirit* (Titus 3:3-5).

We are saved because Jesus is kind. In 2 Samuel 9 is a beautiful illustration of the kindness of God. David is reigning as the king; one day he says, "*Is there yet any that is left of the household of Saul, that I may show him kindness for Jonathan's sake . . . is there not yet any of the house of Saul, that I may show the kindness of God unto him?*" What is *the kindness of God?* It is undeserved favor. Has Saul done anything good to or for David? No, yet David says, "I want to show God's kindness to someone in the house of Saul. I want to give forgiveness." They find Mephibosheth, a lame man who is the son of Jonathan. Because of Jonathan, David shows kindness to Mephibosheth. That is the kindness of God. God is kind to us, not because we are so good but for Jesus' sake—because of the grace of the Lord Jesus Christ. If I am going to forgive, I must show kindness. The *kindness* of God is shown to those who do not deserve it.

B. **Tenderheartedness** is another essential. A hardened heart is a terrible thing. A hardened heart robs you of blessings and joy! A hardened heart is the result of bitterness and anger, wrath and malice. A hardened heart results when we harbor evil feelings inside. Paul makes clear the fact that if we don't have a tender heart, we can never be forgiving.

C. **Honesty** is the third essential mentioned for a forgiving spirit. As already discussed in Matthew 18 Jesus tells Christians how to get along with each other.

> 15 "*Moreover if your brother sins against you, go and tell him his fault between you and him alone. If he hears you, you have gained your brother.*
>
> 16 *But if he will not hear, take with you one or two more, that 'by the mouth of two or three witnesses every word may be established.'*
>
> 17 *And if he refuses to hear them, tell it to the church. But if he refuses even to hear the church, let him be to you like a heathen and a tax collector*" (Matt. 18:15-17).

My experience as a pastor is that when you take the first step, God usually works in the person's heart and the problem gets solved. When saints can be honest with each other in love, the results are wonderful. Do you harbor bitterness down inside? If someone in the church fellowship has done something against you, don't go around talking about it, don't get bitter, and don't develop a hardened heart. Don't think up unkind things to say and do. Go to that person honestly and humbly and try to get it settled. Do you know why? Because "God for Christ's sake has forgiven you!"

At the end of Matthew 18 our Lord tells the parable about the servant who owes the king a great deal of money. The king orders the man and his family to be sold so that the debt can be paid, but the man begs and says, "Please give me time and I will repay you," which he cannot have done in a hundred lifetimes. The king takes pity on him and forgives him the entire debt.

Then the servant meets a man who owes him money—a fraction of what he owes the king. The servant grabs the man by the throat, shakes him, and says, "Pay what you owe me!" The man begs the servant to be patient. He says, "I will pay you if you give me time." But the servant will not give him time; he will not forgive him. When the king hears about this, he is angry and puts the servant into prison because he has not forgiven his fellow servant. Why does the servant not forgive?

Obviously I don't know for sure, but I think this happens because he cannot believe he is really forgiven. Somehow he believes he must attempt to get the money together for the day the king will call for payment again. That is so true today. Many don't feel forgiven; they don't believe experiencing forgiveness is possible, so because they have not experienced the forgiveness of God or they have but can't believe it's real, they can't be forgiving to others. What an agonizing way to live!

Forgiveness is a choice. When I release someone by an act of my will, like God I no longer hold the offense against the person, even though the circumstance may be etched in my memory. God's grace lets its sharpness fade away. While forgiving may be difficult, not forgiving is even tougher. If we don't forgive, we grieve the Holy Spirit. If we don't forgive, we deny what Jesus does for us on the cross. If we don't forgive, we are not walking in love. Ephesians 5:2 says, *And walk in love, as Christ also has loved us and given Himself for us, an offering and a sacrifice to God for a sweet-smelling aroma.* Caring Christians forgive one another. Life is too short to have enemies. Enemies are very expensive. If we are not going to have enemies, we are going to forgive. We are going to forgive, not because anyone deserves it but for Jesus' sake.

Some questions to consider:

1. Examine your conversations throughout a given 24-hour period. What does your speech reveal about you? Do you struggle to eliminate from your conversation unkind references to others? What would you need to do to change these patterns?

2. Do you have difficulty feeling truly forgiven? If so, why? Have you ever considered that this lack of acceptance of forgiveness causes bitterness to infect your heart?

3. Have you ever had difficulty worshiping because you harbored unforgiveness against someone? What did you do about the situation?

4. Can you think of a time in which unforgiveness actually brought on physical illness on you? If so, did you realize at the time that your attitude was at the root of this?

5. Can you think of a time in your experience in which unforgiveness among the brethren was a source of disunity in a church situation? What happened as a result?

6. Describe an experience in which you deliberately, willfully, and volitionally chose to grant forgiveness. Can you testify to the life-changing benefits that forgiving another brings?

7. Have you ever experienced the kindness of God through the mercy of another human being? How does that help you understand the kind of forgiveness you are to extend?

8. Have you ever approached someone and tried a peaceable discussion to settle a matter between the two of you? What happened?

Lesson #9

Submit to One Another

Ephesians 5:21, 1 Peter 5:5

Submitting yourselves one to another in the fear of God (Eph. 5:21).

Likewise, you younger, submit yourselves unto the elder. Yea, all of you be subject to one another, and be clothed with humility. For God resisteth the proud, and gives grace to the humble (1 Pet. 5:5).

We live in an era of self-expression and independence. The slogan of most people seems to be "I'm going to do my thing my way." The theme song of hell is "I did it my way"—just read the lyrics. Yet the Word of God tells us that the way to fulfillment is through submission. This submission is the result of the fullness of the Spirit. *And be not drunk with wine, wherein is excess; but be filled with the Spirit* (Eph. 5:18) How can you tell whether someone is filled with the Holy Spirit? Will the person perform miracles? Will the person's face have some strange glow around it? Will he or she speak in some heavenly language?

According to Paul, three things evidence of the filling of the Holy Spirit. The first is: We are joyful. *Speaking to yourselves in psalms, hymns and spiritual songs, singing and making melody in your heart to the Lord* (Eph. 5:19) Secondly, we are thankful. *Giving thanks always for all things unto God and the Father in the name of our Lord Jesus Christ* (Eph. 5:20). Lastly, we are submitted to one another. *Submitting yourselves one to another in the fear of God* (Eph. 5:21) This whole matter of submission, then, relates to the fullness of the Holy Spirit.

If you and I are walking in the power of the flesh, we will not submit. The flesh is proud; the flesh always wants to assert itself. The New Testament has nothing good to say about the flesh. "*The flesh profiteth nothing*" (John 6:63). If we are walking in the Holy Spirit's power, then we will be joyful, thankful, and submissive.

Please do not reverse that order! We first submit to the Holy Spirit and let Him fill us. To be filled with the Holy Spirit means to be controlled by the Holy Spirit. The Holy Spirit thinks through our minds, loves through our hearts, and acts through our wills as it uses the members of our bodies. To be filled with the Holy Spirit means to be controlled by the Spirit. The result of that filling is that we are joyful, thankful, and submissive.

When people are joyful, they have no problem submitting. When we are thankful, we have no problem submitting, but when we are complaining, criticizing, and thinking we have gotten a raw deal, then we have a tough time submitting. Then we start asserting ourselves to get what we think we really deserve.

When we mention *submission*, we are not talking about subjugation or slavery. We are not talking about bondage. In the local church or in the home should be no slavery or bondage. We have been called into gracious, wonderful liberty. However, this liberty means freedom to submit to each other.

Perhaps a good illustration is the human body. My body is made up of many different members. Each member has a function to perform, but each member depends on the other members. As the members of my body submit to each other, the body functions normally. I feel good; I get my work done. But suppose one member of my body decides not to submit and wants to go its own way; then I have trouble! I may have to go to the doctor; I might even need surgery to correct what is wrong.

The menace

We have many reasons in our culture to resist submitting to anyone or anything. We live in a state of rugged individualism that says, "It's all about me." I love my rights and my entitlements. In our political campaigns the slogan "Country First" has been embraced. To the average citizen that is a new concept.

This sense of individualism has made its way into our theology. The belief of "the priesthood of the believer" has been distorted to mean that the local church should have no authority. The church has never been a democracy run by a show of hands. We will always have God's role as a theocracy and men called to be undershepherds to Great Shepherd, Jesus Christ. Anything with two hands is a minister; anything with no head is dead. The principle of submission is for the church, home, and government.

The biggest opposition to submission is pride. We want anonymity. We don't want people to know our business, especially as it relates to the Lord. "Religion is a private matter" is the cry. OK, but Christianity is not a religion; it's a relationship with Christ and one another. While that is personal, it is everything but private.

The meaning

To submit does not signify blind obedience to another person. The church is not a democracy; neither is it a dictatorship. The word *submit* simply means a lining up under an authority. It has nothing to do with value or importance. The purpose of submitting is for accountability and encouragement, not for lording over or controlling one another. We are the body of Christ; submission is essential.

Jesus was the greatest example of all. He was totally yielded to the Father and submitted to the will, plan, and purpose laid out from the foundation of the world.

The method

It all begins with submission to the Lord. *Therefore as the church is subject unto Christ . . .* (Eph. 5:24). The church must be subject to Christ because Christ is the head of the church. The church is not permitted to go its own way. We must be personally submitted to the Lord. The classic text on that is,

> 1 *I beseech you therefore, brethren, by the mercies of God, that you present your bodies a living sacrifice, holy, acceptable to God, which is your reasonable service.*
>
> 2 *And do not be conformed to this world, but be transformed by the renewing of your mind, that you may prove what is that good and acceptable and perfect will of God* (Rom. 12:1-2).

What does *submitting to the Lord* mean? It means to give Him your body. He wants your body. He has made our bodies

His temple. He also wants our minds. The Word commands us not to be conformed to this world but to be transformed. He also wants our wills . . . *that you may prove what is that good and acceptable and perfect will of God.*

If you want to practice submission, I suggest that every morning you give God your body, your mind, and your will. Ask the Holy Spirit to fill you. That is the beginning of a life of daily victory. First we must submit ourselves to God.

Secondly, we must submit ourselves in the home. Each of us has some relationship, whether we are single or married. The fact that many homes are being destroyed today is too bad. The fact that Satan is permitted to use destructive forces against the home is deplorable. I fear that one of these destructive forces is selfish independence—the kind of independence that is seen in the attitude, "I am going to go my way."

As a pastor, I have seen many homes destroyed. It usually happens this way: A home is founded on the couple making promises to each other and to the Lord. Husband and wife promise to love, honor, and submit. Then somewhere along the way, one of the parties decides he or she wants to go an independent route.

If holiness and happiness are to exist in the home, submission must be there, too. This is not subjugation, not slavery, bondage, or Lordship, but headship—a living, loving relationship. The partners must submit to each other. If a husband is submitted to the Lord and a wife is submitted to the Lord, they have no problem submitting to each other. The wife shows her submission by reverence to and respect for the husband. The husband shows his submission through loving acts and through caring for his wife in love.

Someone might wonder, *Why doesn't Paul say for the husbands to submit*? He does not use the word s*ubmit*, but in Ephesians 5:25 he does say that the husband has a great responsibility; he is supposed to love his wife *as Christ loved the church.* That's the ultimate submission! Christ gave Himself for the church. The husband's love is to be a sacrificial love. He is to sacrifice so that his wife might be able to submit in return.

When this commandment is obeyed and this principle is followed, the home experiences the blessing of God. Once again, this is not slavery; it is a lining up under God's ordained authority. When children obey their parents, they are actually obeying God.

The third area of submission is in the local church. As a pastor I have had many experiences in churches. Finding a church in which people are submitted to each other is a great joy. Too often, however, people in churches debate with each other and disagree or fight with each other. Some churches split; the splits produce splinters, and their testimony for the Lord is hurt.

The principle of submission in the church is described in 1 Peter 5:2-5,

> 2 *Shepherd the flock of God which is among you, serving as overseers, not by compulsion but willingly, not for dishonest gain but eagerly;*
> 3 *nor as being lords over those entrusted to you, but being examples to the flock;*
> 4 *and when the Chief Shepherd appears, you will receive the crown of glory that does not fade away. Likewise you younger people, submit yourselves to your elders. Yes, all of you be submissive to one another, and be clothed with humility, for "God resists the proud, but gives grace to the humble."*

Too bad that we have some sanctified obstructions or persons in church leadership who always have to get their own way. Too bad that some cannot submit, particularly in matters that are simply not that important. Those individuals have to have their say and their way. Submission in the local church is the way to grow. It is the way for God's blessing to occur. It is the way for the Holy Spirit to fall and anoint the work of God in the congregation.

Here is why submission is so important: It is important because God controls our lives. If we do not submit, then other people besides God control our lives.

The person who says, "I'm going to do it my way . . . I'll never submit to an authority", actually spends all his or her time responding and reacting to the resistance of other people. People such as this think they are controlling their lives, but they are not. Other people are controlling them. When we submit, God controls; when we don't submit, then other people control. When we refuse to submit to spiritual authority, we lead a life of misery, fighting, and defensiveness. That's not the kind of life God wants us to live. The Bible says . . . *submitting yourselves one to another in the fear of God* (Eph. 5:21).

Are you a submissive Christian? Being submissive does not mean we lose ourselves; it means we find ourselves. Submissiveness does not mean God is going to cheat us; it means God is going to enrich us!

Some questions to consider:

1. What kind of fine line exists between healthy independence and yielding one's self to the Holy Spirit's influence? How can a person die to self and yet be free of extreme outside influences that steal one's self-identity?

2. What kind of individuality would be healthy in the local church? What kind would be harmful?

3. Why is submission essential in the body of Christ? How can members submit to one another in a healthy way?

4. In what way does God want our bodies submitted to Him?

5. What do you think life would be like for you if every morning you submitted your mind, body, and soul to God? How would your day-to-day existence be different from what it already is if you experienced this kind of submission?

6. What would happen in a marriage if a husband truly loved his spouse as Christ loved the church? What kind of relationship would exist in that home? If you are a husband, what mid-course corrections, if necessary, would you need to make to truly love your spouse as Christ loved the church?

7. Who is in control of your life—God or others? If you are resisting God's authority, under what person's authority do you line up?

8. Describe a time in which you believe you've found yourself by submitting.

Lesson #10

Be Kind to One Another

Romans 12:9-10

> 9 *Let love be without hypocrisy. Abhor what is evil. Cling to what is good.*
> 10 *Be kindly affectionate to one another with brotherly love, in honor giving preference to one another . . .* (Rom. 12:9-10).

Some years ago Glen Campbell had a hit song entitled "Try A Little Kindness." This song reinforced conventional thinking about kindness, as it suggested that with the slightest effort—a good word, a helpful deed, a positive gesture—relationship-saving wonder could be accomplished. Then we saw the movie "Pay It Forward" in which a child envisioned changing the world if one would simply look for ways to show kindness in helpful ways to people needing a helping hand. And then we saw the soft-drink commercial that shows how acts of kindness can inspire others to lift us with a simple deed of kindness.

Clearly you don't have to be a Christian to know what kindness can do in our world. The problem with the illustrations mentioned is that kindness isn't always rewarded so quickly and profusely. When you pay it forward, you may get stabbed in the back, as it were, for your effort. Thus we see the much-quoted proverb, "No good deed goes unpunished."

Kindness is a word that has *eternity* written all over it. To explain some of the distinctions between biblical and conventional thinking on the subject, let us first do some theology. Paul says kindness boils down to preferring one another. We are to glorify God and honor people. Simply put this means that you and I are to be willing for others to get the recognition and to receive honor. This means that we are to be willing not to be recognized at all if doing so is the will of God. Christians are to prefer one another in honor.

What *preferring one another* does not mean

It does not mean **empty flattery**. Today books are available that tell you how to flatter your way into or out of anything. A brand of psychology tells you to find "the hot-button" in every person's life—find out a person's true interests. Then you can use that information to your own advantage. This leads, of course, to manipulating people. Paul is not talking about empty flattery, because in Romans 12:9 he says, *Let love be without hypocrisy.*

We've all seen that this hypocritical kind of love exists—the shallow, gushy type of love that is all words and no deeds. This kind of love is manufactured, artificial, and brittle and does not last. Paul tells us our love for each other is to be sincere and honest. No hypocrisy is to be involved in it. Flattery is something from which Christians must flee.

In 1 Thessalonians 2:5-6 Paul writes,

> 5 *For neither at any time did we use flattering words, as you know, nor a cloak for covetousness—God is witness.*
>
> 6 *Nor did we seek glory from men, either from you*

or from others, when we might have made demands as apostles of Christ.

Paul does not flatter people into the kingdom; he does not flatter people to get something out of them. He does not manipulate people. In Proverbs 26:28 God warns against flattering lips: *A lying tongue hates those who are crushed by it, And a flattering mouth works ruin.*

Secondly, it **does not mean that we belittle ourselves.** Sometimes people have the idea that *in honor preferring one another* means that we have to lie about ourselves and belittle ourselves. These people go around saying "I can't do anything" or "I'm not worth anything." That, of course, is sin. We are worth something. Every believer has spiritual gifts that God has given them, "*For I say, through the grace given unto me, to every man that is among you, not to think of himself more highly than he ought to think, but to think soberly, according as God hath dealt to every man a measure of faith*" (Rom. 12:3). We want to avoid two extremes: we should not think too highly of ourselves, and we must not think too lowly of ourselves.

When God calls Moses, Moses belittles himself. Moses said, "*I am not an eloquent speaker. I am slow to speech*" (Ex. 4:10). He is saying that he is literally clumsy with words. God has to rebuke him and say, "I made your tongue, I made your mouth, now obey me." Belittling yourself is belittling God. Some people go to God's house and say, "Well, I'm not very important. I don't teach a Sunday School class, I'm not on the board, I don't sing in the choir, so I'm not very important." But you are important. All of us are valuable to God and the kingdom work.

> 4 *For as we have many members in one body, but all the members do not have the same function,*
> 5 *so we, being many, are one body in Christ, and individually members of one another.*
> 6 *Having then gifts differing according to the grace that is given to us, let us use them: if prophecy, let us prophesy in proportion to our faith;*
> 7 *or ministry, let us use it in our ministering; he who teaches, in teaching;*
> 8 *he who exhorts, in exhortation; he who gives, with liberality; he who leads, with diligence; he who shows mercy, with cheerfulness* (Rom. 12:4-8).

Paul lists the seven areas of spiritual giftedness. This means not only does God love us and we matter, we are meant to contribute to the kingdom of God. We are to discover our spiritual gifts and use them to the glory of God.

Thirdly, it does not mean **showing partiality**. We all tend to show partiality. Leaders have a tendency to like certain people and to get along better with certain people. We have to be very careful about this. When Paul writes to Timothy to instruct him about the local church, he says, *I charge thee before God, and the Lord Jesus Christ, and the elect angels, that thou observe these things without preferring one before another, doing nothing by partiality* (1 Tim. 5:21).

Preferring one before another is wrong and shows prejudice. This is a difficult principle to practice. Being partial is a very easy situation to fall into, but we are instructed not to do so. We are not to give attention to one person and neglect another.

What *preferring one another* means

It means we put others ahead of ourselves. Philippians 2:3 says, *Let nothing be done through selfish ambition or conceit, but in lowliness of mind let each esteem others better than himself* (Phil. 2:3). Consider the story of Abraham and Lot in Genesis 13. In the story their flocks and herds have multiplied; the land has had a famine; consequently enough pasture isn't available for both of them. Fighting is taking place among the herdsmen. Abraham could have said, "Now, Lot, I am older than you are; I am in charge, therefore, I suggest you go here or you go there." He does not say that. Abraham says, "Now, Lot, if you go to the left, I'll go to the right; if you go to the right, I'll go to the left." He prefers to give the honor to Lot. Lot abuses that privilege, but that is not Abraham's fault. Abraham shows the right spirit.

This is where King Saul gets into trouble. God begins to use David as a warrior. When the soldiers return, the women sing, "*Saul hath slain his thousands, and David his ten thousands*" (1 Sam. 18:7). And what happens? Saul gets envious and jealous. Instead of saying, "Praise God for this warrior," he begins to watch David and looks for a reason to confirm the sinful envy in his heart. He finds an excuse; so will we. Before long Saul's envy turns to hatred; he tries to kill David. We are to give honor where honor is due and give respect where respect is due, all the while giving all the glory and praise to Jesus.

If God is getting the glory, why does whether we receive the credit matter?

> 29 *He who has the bride is the bridegroom; but the friend of the bridegroom, who stands and hears him, rejoices greatly because of the bridegroom's voice.*

Therefore this joy of mine is fulfilled.
30 *He must increase, but I must decrease*
(John 3:29-30).

We can have this humble attitude by only one way. To be kind means having our minds renewed by a revelation from above, our hearts purged from many ulterior motives, and our spirit energized by Almighty God. That's why Samuel says, *Kindness is of the Lord.* It can never be produced in the flesh, no matter how well-meaning it is. Without a divine infusion of His wisdom and strength, our kindness, commended by others though it may be, won't begin to approach the success God could have supplied. Isaiah describes God's kindness as an . . . *everlasting kindness* . . . (Isa. 54:8). This describes a kindness that never gives up, never runs out, and can't be humanly produced.

How to be kind

First we must **have a healthy distrust of our own capacities.** This is precisely what most people don't have. In praying about our own weakness, we give it to God for His Spirit to work through us as it prompts our hearts and empowers our wills.

Secondly, we must **ask for God's wisdom about a particular person**. We not only need to be noble, we need to be wise. We are nobody's source; we are simply vessels for God's love to flow through. Kindness is God's love in action through us. It requires kindness to fulfill the Great Commandment (Matt. 22:39) *And the second is like it: "You shall love your neighbor as yourself."* Showing concern begins by asking questions, because that's how we learn about other people.

Prov. 20:5 says, *Counsel in the heart of man is like deep water, but a man of understanding will draw it out*. We just can't tell what's going on in a person's life by looking at him or her Remember the old 1970s musical hit by Johnny Rivers, "The Tracks of My Tears"? It's about a man who appears to be the life of the party because he is always laughing, but inside he actually is very sad. The song says, "Take a good look at my face . . .." We can see "the tracks of his tears." When we see the tracks of tears in someone's life, be sensitive and be cordial; listen to the person and hear with your ears and your eyes. Body language is a real way people communicate. Remember, *Anxiety in the heart of man causes depression, but a good word makes it glad* (Prov. 12:25). Kindness is more than niceness; it is the act of deliberately, purposefully being nice. In this crude, rude world, Christians are to share the light of kindness by being nice. Being kind by being nice actually pays. *The merciful man does good for his own soul, but he who is cruel troubles his own flesh* (Prov. 11:17).

I heard the story of a man who told the server in a coffee shop, "I want a cup of coffee and a donut, and step on it." The server returned with coffee and a donut which was flattened. He asked, "What happened to my donut?" She replied, "You told me to step on it." Kindness speaks life into people. *There is one who speaks like the piercings of a sword, but the tongue of the wise promotes health* (Prov. 12:18).

If we are to practice kindness, we have to be determined and intentional. This requires us to stay focused on the result of kindness. God is our kindness to bring about repentance and change in others. In 1 Peter 3 Peter tells us that an unbelieving husband is convicted by kindness in the wife's life. My grandmother used to say, "Deeds of kindness heap coals of fire on other's hearts." The reality is that when we are kind, we improve the atmosphere and God can be at work through us.

Paul says in Colossians 3:12 that Christians are to be clothed with five qualities of God; kindness is among them. Kindness is part of the basic clothing of a Christian. If we are not kind, we are not properly dressed in God's sight.

We are to be kind in two places:

1. Be kind in private. Kindness will pay no greater dividends than in the home. How some people can be kind in public but so mean at home is amazing. However, "believer-building" begins in our homes. That's why God gives a warning to those who don't work to support their families. First Timothy 5:8 says, *But if anyone does not provide for his own, and especially for those of his household, he has denied the faith and is worse than an unbeliever.* We are to provide more for our families than just the physical realities. We are to provide a kind environment in our homes. How sad that family violence is not limited to a pagan culture; it is in the homes of believers. This is such a disgrace to God. This is not limited to violent fathers; it is also seen in screaming mothers.

2. Be kind in public. This means in traffic on the interstate and in line at Wal-Mart. We can't find justification for what's going on in our culture. Can you believe we even have a term called *road rage* to identify our behavior? In speaking to some college kids who wait on tables at restaurants, they will tell you some of the most unloving people they serve are believers. Most try to avoid serving tables on Sunday, not only because they want to be in church, but also because they don't want to wait on churchgoers. They say, "Christians are for the most part demanding and cheap in tipping."

> 6 *But this I say: He who sows sparingly will also reap sparingly, and he who sows bountifully will also reap bountifully* (2 Cor. 9:6).

Some questions to consider:

1. Have you ever allowed someone else to get the honor for something in which you truly deserved the lion's share of credit? What happened when you did?

2. How do you sin if you belittle yourself? What does thinking *soberly* of one's self mean? Why do we sometimes equate self-deprecating with godliness?

3. How can you work to avoid partiality in the work setting? in the home? in the church setting? What can partiality lead to?

4. Think of a time in which you have put another ahead of yourself. Why do we resist doing this? How can you defer to another person while at the same time make sure that others do not take advantage of your deference?

5. Think of a time in which you have truly rejoiced selflessly in another's successes. How did doing so make you feel? Why is this sometimes difficult to do?

6. When you realize that kindness can't be humanly practiced without God's empowering, what would be necessary for you to "program in" to your life a pattern of asking God to empower you to be kind to certain others?

7. The lesson commends the practice of asking questions of another as part of fulfilling God's love in action. How active are you in doing this? Had you realized that asking questions of another is actually a means of showing kindness? What keeps you from this practice?

8. How do you rate your acts of kindness in the home setting? Why is kindness in this setting difficult to do?

9. How are you as a restaurant tipper? a customer in the grocery line? a parent in a child's school setting? a spectator at a sports game? a driver behind the wheel? a church member?

Lesson 11

Show Hospitality to One Another
1 Peter 4:7-10

7 *But the end of all things is at hand; therefore be serious and watchful in your prayers.*
8 *And above all things have fervent love for one another for "love will cover a multitude of sins."*
9 *Be hospitable to one another without grumbling.*
10 *As each one has received a gift, minister it to one another, as good stewards of the manifold grace of God* (1 Pet. 4:7-10).

So often people forget that hospitality is a gift from God. To a great hurt our culture has lost the desire and practice of hospitality. We now live in a generation that is more concerned about getting away from home than being at home. The kind of old-fashioned Christian hospitality we once saw is disappearing from the life of the church. How tragic this is! Our homes are to be places of ministry to serve God. We have bigger and nicer homes and spend less and less time there. Kitchens are equipped with the latest, most convenient appliances, but they are used less and less. We often justify buying our dream homes by saying we can use these for God's work, but we rarely open up our homes for this type of service.

Yet, fellowship is a wonderful vehicle for evangelism. God wants His people to have open hands, open hearts, and open doors. In Romans 12:13 Paul says, *We are to be given to hospitality.* That is, we're to have a knack for it, a desire for it, a time set aside for it, and a budget for it. Paul tells Titus that we are to be *lovers of hospitality*—not lovers on the receiving end only but on the giving end of hospitality.

The reality is that the church is filled with members that are strangers to one another. People want to attend a friendly church. We, like Wal-Mart, can hire friendly people. People want to attend a church in which they have friends.

The larger the church's attendance, the more diligently Christians must work on hospitality. That's why Bible Life classes are at the heart of what God is doing to evangelize the lost and edify the believer. In our busy world we have two major hindrances—motivation and time: motivation because sometimes spending time with people is just one more thing we have to squeeze into our lives and time because we are horrible at time management.

Three facts about hospitality

It is **an important ministry**—so important that Paul, in giving the qualifications of a bishop, tells Timothy that he is to be *hospitable*. The same word is used in Titus 1:8. Those who lead in ministry must understand that hospitality opens doors as few other things do. We often say that every member is a minister; therefore, every one of God's children needs to be involved in the ministry of hospitality.

The phrase *given to hospitality* means that it is to be habitual. It is not an obligation, it's an opportunity. Believers are to yield themselves to it; they are to become addicted to it, so to speak. They are to open their homes to the glory of God.

The Christian's home is to be a haven on earth. Charles

Haddon Spurgeon said, "When home is ruled according to God's Word, angels might be asked to stay with us, and they would not find themselves out of their element." Isn't that an interesting statement? Would angels feel at home in your home or mine?

God has established only three institutions in this world—human government, the church, and the home. In the Bible, when God brings Adam and Eve together and performs, as it were, the first marriage ceremony in Eden, He establishes the first home. The home is the first and holiest.

One verse we usually think of in terms of hospitality is Hebrews 13:2, *Do not forget to entertain strangers, for by so doing some have unwittingly entertained angels.* Abraham does that (see Gen. 18:1-22). One day while Abraham is resting, he sees three strangers traveling down the road. He does not know who they are. Some of the pictures we see of this scene have halos over the heads of these people. While two of them appear to be angels, the other one appears to be the Lord Jesus. That's probably not accurate. The fact that they are angels is not obvious, even through that's who they are.

The word *angels* means messengers. Did you know your guest may be God's messenger? What you have to offer the guest may not be crucial; what the person has to offer you may be what's so important.

No one studying the Book of Acts can miss how God uses hospitality in the early church. It was a vital part of the church.

> 5 *Beloved, you do faithfully whatever you do for the brethren and for strangers,*
>
> 6 *who have borne witness of your love before the church. If you send them forward on their journey in a manner worthy of God, you will do well,*
>
> 7 *because they went forth for His name's sake, tak-*

ing nothing from the Gentiles.

8 *We therefore ought to receive such, that we may become fellow workers for the truth* (3 John 1:5-8).

Hospitality is considered by God **a faithful ministry**. We help the truth of God to go forth by showing hospitality and by taking care of those who minister. In these days of increasing economic pressure, we need to be giving more attention to this vital ministry.

Hospitality **brings blessings**! The law of the harvest includes this act. Luke 6:38 says, *Give, and it will be given to you: good measure, pressed down, shaken together, and running over will be put into your bosom. For with the same measure that you use, it will be measured back to you.*

God loves for us to share. Doing so is part of our stewardship.

35 "*for I was hungry and you gave Me food; I was thirsty and you gave Me drink; I was a stranger and you took Me in;*

36 *I was naked and you clothed Me; I was sick and you visited Me; I was in prison and you came to Me.*

37 *Then the righteous will answer Him, saying, 'Lord, when did we see You hungry and feed You, or thirsty and give You drink?*

38 *When did we see You a stranger and take You in, or naked and clothe You?*

39 *Or when did we see You sick, or in prison, and come to You?'*

40 *And the King will answer and say to them, 'Assuredly, I say to you, inasmuch as you did it to one of the least of these My brethren, you did it to Me'*" (Matt. 25:35-40).

Attitude adjustments

In 1 Peter 4:1 Peter reminds us of how Jesus *suffered for us*. That is, leaving His home in glory where everything was absolutely perfect, Jesus descended to this little spinning dot of rebellion to save us. We have no way to quantify and qualify the suffering Jesus endured to accomplish this, but we do know that His suffering was a lot more than what any of us deserved. Therefore, being the ones who gain from such an enormous suffering, are we now going to shut our hearts and refuse to pass on to others what was so graciously given to us?

In 1 Peter 4:2 Peter points out that we're no longer to live in the flesh *for the lusts of men, but for the will of God*. This speaks of lordship—the principle being, because Jesus died on our behalf, we are now to live on His behalf. This seems fair. After all, if we were to go back in time and reconsider our surrender to the Lord, we would have to conclude that this is the best decision we could have ever made! For who would want to have the enemy inside (self), the enemy outside (Satan), and the enemy all around (the world) to regain their advantage? Who would want to be living life on a collision course with God, knowing that one is only a heartbeat away from hell? And who would want to face every problem alone with no promises on which to count, no wisdom greater than his or her own, and no intervening help if ever it should be needed?

Life under new management is good news. If God is calling us to a ministry of hospitality, then despite the inconvenience this might bring or entail for the moment, we are to quickly obey. We can realize that even if we were looking at this challenge from a strictly selfish point of view, the very best thing we can do is exactly what God says.

First Peter 4:3 reminds us of what the old life was like—the lewdness, the lust, the drunkenness. The world calls this *having a good time*, but if a video of one of the world's parties could be reviewed the next day, a good case could be made that really, the devil is the one who is having a good time at their expense! If having a good time means ending up with a splitting headache the next morning and of being positioned on all four sides of the toilet, this has got to be a very warped view of what constitutes a good time.

God wants his church to give the world a far better example. The hospitality of His church is to far exceed the revelry and rioting of the world because it is Spirit-led and not flesh-driven.

Jesus is ready to re-enter history. While we don't know the hour or the day, we are told to make all our decisions in the light of His glorious face.

Some questions to consider:

1. Most Christians would probably acknowledge that they are not the "lovers of hospitality" that God wants them to be. Identify the first step you would need to make in order for your love to become more fervent.

2. Of all the motives for hospitality given in 1 Peter 4, which one speaks to you the most?

3. Which way of hospitality is most suitable to you?

4. What strategy could your class use to make hospitality a more effective evangelistic vehicle?

5. Why do we view hospitality as a drudgery and a cross to bear rather than a gift from God to exercise freely?

6. Do you set aside time for hospitality and budget for it? If not, why not?

7. Can you think of a time in which someone's act of hospitality made a difference in how welcome you felt in a new

church setting? If so, what did someone do to make this happen?

8. Why do we sometimes believe that spending time with people is just one more thing on our to-do lists? What would be necessary to make this activity seem less burdensome?

9. How can you be hospitable in ways that extend beyond the home? How might this ministry apply to welcoming visitors to your Bible-study class? to worship services? being receptive to those in your day-to-day life who might be different from you? being receptive to those who visit your church who might be different from you?

10. Could your home be described as a *haven on earth*—the statement the lesson makes about the Christian's home? If not, what adjustments need to be made to make this description apt?

Lesson 12

Lie Not to One Another

Colossians 3:8-11

8 *But now you yourselves are to put off all these:
anger, wrath, malice, blasphemy, filthy language out of
your mouth.*
9 *Do not lie to one another, since you have put off
the old man with his deeds,*
10 *and have put on the new man who is renewed in
knowledge according to the image of Him who created
him.*
11 *where there is neither Greek nor Jew, circum-
cised nor uncircumcised, barbarian, Sicythian, slave
nor free, but Christ is all and in all* (Col. 3:8-11).

God takes our words seriously. One day believers will stand before the judgment seat of Christ. Our works and our words will be examined. The judgment seat of Christ is not a judgment as we typically think of judgment but rather a review for rewarding. Every believer will go to heaven, but the judgment seat is a place of examination. The Bible says we will give an account for every idle word we have spoken. The ninth commandment says, "*Thou shalt not bear false witness*" (Ex. 20:16). This same commandment is repeated in Romans 13:9 and John 8:44. We are told Satan is a liar and the father of all lies. In Proverbs 6:16-17 we are told that God hates liars. In fact, in Revelation 21:8, 27 and 22:15 God informs us that liars will have their places in hell.

God can forgive our sins; we all know this. The Apostle Peter does not tell the truth when he denies our blessed Lord, yet he is forgiven. Often you and I are under the same kind of pressure. We succumb to temptation and tell what we often call a "white lie"—a half-truth. Our hearts convict us, we confess it, and God forgives us. But God takes lying seriously.

Someone has said that one of the most deceiving lies a liar tells is that he doesn't tell lies. The very nature of lying is not to be aware of how frequently we resort to it. Oliver Wendell Holmes once said, "Sin has many tools, but a lie is the handle which fits them all." The preponderance of lies in our culture is owing to this connection with other sin—lies that justify the necessity of the sin, that minimize the extent of the sin, that hide the face of sin. Our world sometimes seems to run on lies. Salesmen are trained to lie. Politicians are schooled in the fine art of lying. How do you know whether a politician is lying? You see if his mouth is moving! That's culture's commentary on that vocation. Religious people lie. The Koran teaches that lying is permissible if the lie will have a good outcome. Hindus permit five kinds of lies:

- Lies relating to marriage.
- Lies for gratification or lust.
- Lies to save a life.
- Lies to protect prosperity.
- Lies to protect a holy man.

Christians do not believe in lying, yet we often practice lying. A little boy in Sunday School was asked, "What is a lie?" In his best voice the little boy said, "A lie is an abomination unto the Lord and our everpresent help in time of trouble."

What is a *lie*?

I suppose the simplest definition would be that a *lie* is a deliberate and conscious misrepresentation of the truth. A lie has to be deliberate; it is not an accident. If you ask me to tell the time and my watch is not working properly, I would give you the wrong time but not deliberately. I am not deliberately trying to misrepresent the truth. Sometimes we fail to tell the truth by accident; sometimes we are ignorant of the truth. But a lie represents a deliberate intent to deceive; our motive is to deceive.

We can lie just by saying things in a certain way. The inflection of our voices could make people believe that we mean something else. We can lie with our lips; we can lie with our lives. What we say, why we say it, and the way we say it determines whether or not our words are truth. A lie is a deliberate and conscious misrepresentation of the truth.

Why do we lie?

Wouldn't telling the truth just be easier? I believe that Abraham Lincoln said, "If a man is going to be a liar, he had better have a good memory." That advice has a great deal of truth in it.

Sometimes we lie out of pride; we want to impress people. In Acts 5 Ananias and Sapphira tried to lie to God and did lie to the church because they wanted to impress people. Barnabas had given a gift to the church; Ananias and Sapphira thought they would get in on some of the honor, but they lied. I don't know why we think we have to impress people. The only person we really have to please is the Lord.

Sometimes we lie because of fear; we don't want to be discovered. Before we sin, Satan says, "No one will know; go ahead and do it." After we sin, Satan says, "Everyone will know, so you need to cover it up!" Now, WE are hiding something; we want to escape the punishment, consequence, and trouble. The poet Sir Walter Scott well stated, "Oh what a tangled web we weave, when first we practice to deceive." Can you remember when you were just a child and you told a lie? Then you had to tell another lie to cover up the first one. Before long you were really in trouble. We lie because we are afraid of being exposed.

Sometimes we lie out of hatred; we want to hurt people. We know gossip does not have to be true; it just has to be repeated enough times. We can make things up; people are eager to believe our words without even determining the truth of the statement. We typically are happy to believe the worst about people.

I think at the bottom of all lying is unbelief. We really don't believe that truth is the best way. Jesus said, "*I am . . . the truth*" (John 14:6). The Holy Spirit is the spirit of truth (John 16:13). God's Word is truth (John 17:17). God Himself is the God of truth (Deut. 32:4). God always blesses truth.

Sometimes truth seems to get us into trouble. That's only temporary; ultimately truth will prevail. When you doubt God's Word and say that you better lie and get out of something, stop! God will bless truth. We lie because of pride, fear, hatred, and unbelief.

To whom do we lie?

Of course we lie to one another. This is so easy to do, because other people are not able to read our minds and hearts. We lie to one another by exaggeration: "You never do this, you always do that!" We have to be very careful not to fall into the trap of exaggeration. Sometimes announcements are exaggerated; sometimes reports are exaggerated. We might even exaggerate statistics.

Sometimes we flatter one another. That's a form of lying. We can even lie when we're singing in church: "All that thrills my soul is Jesus . . .." The young man sings while his hands are all over the girl beside him. We sing, "I'll go where you want me to go, dear Lord," and refuse to return to Sunday-evening services or participate in outreach. "I'll be what you want me to be," and yet in our hearts we have no desire to do anything God wants us to do. Through singing a soloist, a church member, or an entire congregation can lie in church.

We sometimes lie with our testimonies. We speak of how God has been with us and taught us not to fear and to trust completely in His will. We say that we have learned that God's plans and purposes are good and yet live in the fear of bad news for our lives. This is easy to preach and very difficult to live out. We lie in our praying. We pray, "Lord, help us meet the needs of ministry", yet we know we have no intention of sacrificially giving toward the need.

We lie to ourselves. First John 1 tells us that a progressive degeneration begins when we start lying. Verse 6 says, *If we say that we have fellowship with Him, and walk in darkness, we lie and do not practice the truth.* We lie to other people. Verse 8 says, *If we say that we have no sin, we deceive ourselves.* Now we are lying to ourselves. Some Christians who are walking in darkness actually believe they are in the light. They have sin in their lives, but they are lying to themselves and convincing themselves that it really is not sin.

Finally, in verse 10 we read, *If we say that we have not sinned, we make him a liar.* Now we are trying to lie to God! Did you know you really cannot lie to God? We can try. In the

Bible story, Ananias and Sapphira try to lie, but God knows their hearts. God knows the thoughts and the intents of the heart.

How should we tell the truth?

We don't ask why we should tell the truth; we know why—because God commands us to speak truthfully. We are a new creation; we have put off the old life with its lies.

Remember what Colossians 3:9 10 says,

> 9 *Do not lie to one another, since you have put off the old man with his deeds,*
> 10 *and have put on the new man who is renewed in knowledge according to the image of Him who created him . . ..*

As we grow in grace and in the knowledge of our Lord Jesus Christ, we put off the old and put on the new. The new person—the new creation enjoying newness of life—has to practice truth. So we don't ask, "Why should we tell the truth?" We ask how we should do it.

To begin with we are to tell the truth in love. Ephesians 4:15 says, *but, speaking the truth in love, may grow up in all things into Him who is the head—Christ . . ..* (Eph. 4:15). Always speak the truth in love. Don't use the truth as a weapon to hurt someone. Use the truth as a vehicle to build up somebody.

When I go to the dentist, he is tender and gentle. When he drills, he gives me something to numb the pain. I appreciate that! In the same way we are to speak the truth in love.

We should also speak the truth with grace. *Let your speech always be with grace, seasoned with salt, that you may know how you ought to answer each one* (Col. 4:6). Gracious speech springs from a heart that is filled with the grace of our Lord Jesus Christ and that is seasoned with salt. Never say to someone, "Now take this with a grain of salt." You put the salt in it! Salt means purity. Salt means that the statement contains no corruption. When you speak to others, speak graciously and with purity. Employ diplomacy. Think before you speak. Ask yourself, "What is the most thoughtful possible way to state this? If I were the hearer, how would I appreciate the speaker phrasing this message?" Remember the Golden Rule. Consider that other person as you wish to be considered. Avoid placing a burden on the individual simply because you didn't weigh your words carefully enough.

Finally, speak in the name of Jesus.

> 16 *Let the word of Christ dwell in you richly in all wisdom, teaching and admonishing one another in psalms and hymns and spiritual songs, singing with grace in your hearts to the Lord.*
>
> 17 *And whatever you do in word or deed, do all in the name of the Lord Jesus, giving thanks to God the Father through Him* (Col. 3:16-17).

If you can't say something in the name of and to the glory of the Lord Jesus Christ, then don't say it at all.

Lie not one to another. How wonderful if all of us would start being honest with God in our praying and in our worship and start being honest with one other! In ministry team meetings, in church conferences, in worship services, in our Bible studies, and in our conversations, practice honesty and truthfulness.

Some questions to consider:

1. Can you think of a time in which your words made a promise to God that you had absolutely no intention of keeping? How did you feel when you realized this action was a lie to God?

2. How do you feel when you realize that someday when you stand before the judgment seat of Christ, you will have to give an account for each and every lie you have told in your life? What might this reminder motivate you to do?

3. Have you ever had the experience of wanting to withdraw a remark minutes after you uttered it because you realized it was poorly and hurtfully phrased? What would be necessary to help you spend more time cautiously editing your speech before you voice your remarks?

4. Can you recall instances in which you have lied by exaggeration? by flattery? What was the result? At the time this happened, were you aware that your exaggerated or insincere words were tantamount to lies?

5. What is a statement of your faith walk that, deep inside your heart, you know you do not sincerely believe? At what time have your words stated your full confidence in God yet your heart attitude did not support your words? At the time did you recognize this as being untruthful to God?

6. Have you ever used the truth as a club to hurt someone, under the guise the wrongful interpretation of speaking the truth in love? What happened?

7. What steps could you take to be a more truthful Christian? Where does this lesson hit home the most? Can you sincerely pray that the Holy Spirit will prompt you when you are tempted to misstate facts or to try to deceive others or God?

Lesson 13

Pray for One Another

James 5:16

Confess your trespasses to one another, and pray for one another, that you may be healed. The effective, fervent prayer of a righteous man avails much (Jas. 5:16).

The depth of our fellowship experience can be measured by the frequency and fervency of our prayers. This criterion holds true not only in our relationship with God but also in our relationships with other believers. We acknowledge that we easily meet with our fellowship groups each week and talk up a storm. We can share feelings, give advice, teach, exhort, and comfort, but if that's as far as things go, then our part in this fellowship is shallow at best.

A deeper commitment would have us praying, not just as casual, "God-bless-the-church" prayers but also what the Bible would call an *intercessory prayer*. Intercessory prayer begins with an intense focusing on the needs of another person until your own heart is strongly moved. As you visualize that person and see from God's perspective both his or her condition and the Lord's provision, you then will stand in the gap. You will prevail on God to release for your friend that needed grace supply which, surely and supernaturally, will meet his or her need.

Since all the Lord's blessings are released through expectant prayer, we make sense when we say that true love will take up another's need, especially if the person is too weak spiritually to secure the blessing himself or herself. And yet, how little this happens! Christians who say they love each other amazingly will omit the most loving and effective thing they could ever do—the prayer of intercession.

Isaiah cries, "*There is no intercession . . .* " (Isa. 59:16). I sometimes feel that way. James 3 commands that Christians pray for each other. James himself is labeled, "Old camel knees," because his knees have become disfigured from his spending so much time interceding in prayer. Paul says, "*I do not cease to pray for you*" (Col. 1:9). So why does this consistency in prayer occur? Because *the fervent prayer of the righteous man availeth much.*

The responsibility to pray

John Wesley was correct in his observation, "God does nothing but in answer to prayer." God not only has given to us the power of choice but the choice that has power. By praying and praising back His Word with enforcing faith, we can dramatically alter the course of our own lives as well as the lives of others.

Isaiah said that the Word of God would not return void—that is, it will do everything it said it would do. But have you ever stopped to think how the Word is returned at all? It gets returned whenever a believer makes a claim on it, stands on it, believes God for it, and just like Jacob clinging onto the angel, won't let God go until His blessing occur.

What must be made clear is this: just because the Bible makes a promise doesn't mean that promise will be fulfilled in our lives. Moreover, just because we read the promise, understand the promise, and even memorize the promise, this still doesn't mean that that promise will be fulfilled in our lives. Every promise has a condition—a premise. The promise won't be fulfilled until a believer releases a spirit of expectancy within that says, "I have faith to believe God in this. I am making a withdrawal from the bank of hope, where all that I believe about God has been stashed away. I am fully believing that the God of today is going to be as faithful to me as the God of yesterday was to His people in the Bible."

Prayer is not conditioning our minds with wishful thoughts or directing our emotions to some phantom ideal; prayer is a dynamic that has more in common with those businesses that require two signatures before a check will be honored. God has already signed His name to every promise intended for the New Testament believer; now you have to put your name on it also. By your putting your name to it, this means that your entire being—your mind, your will, and your emotions are resting in the Lord's faithfulness to be true to His Word.

Now, we realize when intercessory prayer is concerned, it can never guarantee someone else's response. Jesus stood outside Jerusalem and wept, "*Oh, Jerusalem, Jerusalem! How often I would have gathered you under my wings like a hen gathers its baby chick, but you would not.*" In love Jesus was willing, but people were not. People could resist Jesus' prayers; they can and often do ours.

Prayer does create an atmosphere which better enables God to do His work; therefore, we are responsible for making sure that such an atmosphere exists.

We find we can more easily substitute praying for people by doing the following:

- We sympathize.
- We give advice.
- We dole out money, time, and energy.
- We extend encouragement.

These are good and wonderful things, but they never can replace prayer.

The opposition to prayer

Interceding is tough because it requires sacrifice. Satan slinks around prayer closets to discourage and distract.

The fact is that most Christians, if they are honest, would say, "I don't know how to pray." That's OK, because neither did the disciples. They asked Jesus to "*Teach us to pray.*" Jesus gave them the model prayer. This prayer is not simply to be recited but to be used and understood to gain insight into the ministry of praying. Jesus gives us a guide for prayer,

> *9 "In this manner, therefore, pray: Our Father in heaven, hallowed be Your name.*
>
> *10 Your kingdom come. Your will be done on earth as it is in heaven.*
>
> *11 Give us this day our daily bread.*
>
> *12 And forgive us our debts, as we forgive our debtors.*
>
> *13 And do not lead us into temptation, but deliver us from the evil one. For Yours is the kingdom and the power and the glory forever. Amen.*
>
> *14 For if you forgive men their trespasses, your heavenly Father will also forgive you.*
>
> *15 But if you do not forgive men their trespasses, neither will your Father forgive your trespasses"* (Matt. 6:9-15).

Each phrase gives insight and direction into praying.

"Our Father which art in heaven . . . "

As a believer you are God's child. We have a nearness and intimacy with God as our "Heavenly Father." That means He is a perfect father. As a perfect father—

- He is forgiving (1 John 1:8).
- He is tender-hearted (Ps. 103:13-14).
- He is merciful (Ps. 66:18).
- He answers our requests (1 John 5:14-15).

NOTE: God gives His ear to our prayers if—

- The requester is in God's will (1 John 3:21-23).
- The request is in God's will (Jas. 4:3).
- We ask (Matt. 7:7).

Simply put, when my prayers are in accordance with Scripture, they are exemplified by Jesus Christ. The Holy Spirit will give me peace about it.

"Hallowed be thy name . . . "

As believers we can pray in faith, because God's names represent promised benefits. We therefore are to honor and revere God's names.

Benefit	Name	Meaning
Sin	Jehovah-Tsidkenu	"Jehovah our righteousness"
	Jehovah-M'Kaddesh	"Jehovah who sanctifies"
Spirit	Jehovah-Shalom	"Jehovah is peace"
	Jehovah-Hammah	"Jehovah is there"
Soundness	Jehovah-Rophe	"Jehovah heals"
Success	Jehovah-Jireh	"Jehovah provides"
	Jehovah-Nissi	"Jehovah is my banner"
Security	Jehovah-Rohi	"Jehovah is my shepherd"

"Thy kingdom come—thy will be done"

- Be preoccupied with God's program and plan.
- Our prayer cannot center on ourselves.

- Pray God's will for our lives, families, church, and nation.
- Love only God and hate only sin.

"Give us this day our daily bread"

- Pray for necessities (Prov. 30:8-9).
- "God, I acknowledge that all my sustenance is from you."
- "God, you are owner of all I have, of me, and what you own you provide for."

"Forgive us our debts as we forgive our debtors"

- Prayer should be confession. At salvation we experience judicial forgiveness that saves from sin, but one needs that parental forgiveness that keeps alive the intimate relationship with God our Father.
- As we forgive others, God is likewise forgiving us. He restores joy and intimate fellowship.
- Knowing how God has forgiven me, how can I not forgive others?

"Lead us not into temptation, but deliver us from evil."

- "God, I live in a fallen world; you are my only hope for victory."
- "God, glorify yourself in me; make me a pleasure unto yourself."

Principles of prayer
Daniel 9:1-19

I. Prayer is to be a response to God's Word.

A. When Daniel read the Word, he saw the certainty of divine sovereign purpose and the necessity of prayer.

B. If you don't study God's Word, you can't understand the purpose of God to govern and guide your prayers.

C. Prayer is the means by which believers line themselves up with God's Word and His will.

II. Prayer is realized in self-denial.

A. Daniel's prayer life had no self-seeking in it.

B. He made no demands of God.

C. It involves setting your will aside for God's will.

III. Prayer is identified with God's people.

A. Daniel's prayer was made up of words such as *we, our,* and *us*.

B. His prayer centered on people.

C. He prayed specifically.

IV. Prayer is strengthened in confession.

A. True prayer has a longing for righteousness.

B. It cries for holiness.

C. Prayer rebels against sin.

D. It makes us sensitive and ashamed of sin.

E. It recognizes our responsibility for our sin.

F. It vindicates God when He moves in judgment; it is acknowledging God's right to do so.

V. Prayer depends on God's character.

A. God is a God of great power. "*What is impossible with Man is possible with God.*"

B. God is majesty. He alone is worthy of praise and worship.

C. God is faithful. He will keep His Word. God is a constant God.

Prayer directives from God's Word

1. Prayer for the harvest (Matt. 9:38; Luke 10:2).
2. Pray for the church that it will exalt God on earth (Isa. 62:7).
3. Pray God will open doors of ministry (Col. 4:3).

4. Pray for those who mistreat you (Luke 6:28).
5. Pray that your love will abound toward all men and be pleasure to God. (Phil. 1:9).
6. Pray we will live so that we will be preserved blameless until the Lord comes (1 Thess. 5:23).
7. Pray to have the desires God wants you to have (Ps. 37:4; Mark 11:24).

The enabling of prayer

Neither intelligence nor diligence can put us on the Lord's wavelength. True prayer occurs wherever the Holy Spirit breathes a prayer in us and then bears it to the throne room of the universe.

> "The content of all prayer originates in the heart of God. So it is he who inspires the prayer in the heart of man, and the answer to every God-inspired petition is already prepared before the prayer is uttered. When we are convinced of this, then faith for the answer is easy, far easier than it would be otherwise."—Paul Billheimer

How do you know God's heart? Be a student of the Word of God that reveals the will of God. Be a part of a church that believes and teaches that the Bible is the infallible and inerrant Word of God.

Some questions to consider:

1. What is the current state of your personal prayer life?
2. Discuss how keeping a prayer diary helps you pray more

regularly and more specifically. This also helps you know when God answers your prayer because you are praying specifically. Give your personal testimony about recognizing answered prayer from reviewing your prayer diary.

3. How can your small group be more accountable to intercede for the church? Name some specific ways.

4. Have you ever thought about the fact that the quality of your fellowship with others occurs in direct relationship to the frequency and fervency of your prayer for them? Can you discuss an experience that gives testimony to this in your life?

5. Why do you think you forget to intercede for others about whom you genuinely care? What could help you remember to more readily follow through on your promises to pray for individuals within your sphere of influence?

6. What would be necessary for the phrase *old camel knees* (that the lesson used to describe James) to be used to describe you? How could you develop this kind of intrepid prayer life?

7. When have you substituted advice, money, time, energy, and encouragement toward someone for praying for that person? What would have to happen in your life for you to think of prayer *first* as the *best* means of helping someone?

8. Can you testify as to how you have experienced Satan's slinking around your prayer closest, as the lesson describes, to discourage and distract you from prayer?

9. Can you tell about a specific time in which you have called on one of the names of God the lesson mentioned and have seen one of the benefits promised in that specific name?

10. Read the story of Daniel from Daniel 9:1-19. Describe one lesson about prayer you learned from it.

11. How do you feel when you read Billheimer statement (from your lesson) that prayer originates in God's heart and that He is the One who inspires the prayer in our hearts? Does that make you feel any different about how you are to pray?